Seduction ??
A Biblical Response

Including 1000 verses of Scripture

by Thomas Reid and Mark Virkler
James A. Laine and Alan Langstaff

Foreword by Richard L. Watson
(Dean of Graduate School of Education, Oral Roberts University)

Preface by Florence K. Biros
Introduction by Dr. Thomas F. Reid

CONTAINING:
Eight Critiques of the Seduction of Christianity including
Richard W. Dortch, Robert S. Sterling-Smith,
William L. de Arteaga, John Hurston

PLUS FOUR CONCORDANCE STUDIES:

1. How God Uses Vision and Image
2. Becoming Expressions of God
3. A Positive Mental Attitude and The Word of God
4. Worldview and Advancing Light

"Daniel saw a dream and visions **in his mind....I kept looking** *in the night visions, and behold, with the clouds of heaven One like* **a Son of Man** *was coming, and He came up to* **the Ancient of Days** *and was presented before Him." (Dan. 7:1,13)*

Our gratitude to Carole Williams for her devotion to her Lord and her diligence in helping compile this book along with Mark W. Virkler, The Buffalo School of the Bible, C.F. Swyers & Sons, Inc., Printing, of Buffalo, New York and Don Pratt.

The viewpoints presented here are not necessarily those of either all the authors or the publisher, but are given here to help you discern truth from error. Let the Holy Spirit lead you into the real truth.

Scripture quotations in concordance studies are from the King James Version of the Holy Bible.

"SEDUCTION?? A BIBLICAL RESPONSE"

Copyright © 1986 by Son-Rise Publications and Distribution Co.

Library of Congress Cataloging in Publication Data

ISBN 0-936369-02-7

This book also available from K. Dimension Publishers, Atlanta, GA, Whitaker House, Springdale, PA.

SON-RISE
Publications & Distribution Co.
Rte. 3, P.O. Box 202   New Wilmington, PA 16142

412-946-8334
Revised 7/86   Printed in U.S.A.

FOREWORD

I am extremely pleased to write the foreword to this book. My spirit was grieved by **The Seduction Of Christianity;** beyond grief, I was perplexed by it.

Many Christians today recognize that any biblical truth developed or enunciated apart from God is destructive. Each of us needs, therefore, to be ever vigilant and introspective of our basic motives. I find that to be a major effort in my Christian walk. I, likewise, am repulsed by the notion that I should be providing that service for others. I may be my brother's keeper, but I am not his spiritual evaluator.

It should also be apparent that one of the devil's finest devices is to counterfeit our central value system. The same is true for destroying a ministry. If your ministry is based on agape love, Satan attempts to exchange man as source for God as source. When this is accomplished, agape love becomes lust. If he can get you to substitute man for God in the seed-faith principal, he can turn one of God's basic processes into self-centered materialism. God must be kept on the throne of every ministry and every Christian life. When this relationship is lost, the body of Christ is weakened. Therefore, one must continuously go back to Scripture if God is to rule and direct.

The Hunt and McMahon book conjectures that man is being substituted for God as source in some specifically identified belief systems within the body of Christ today. That is, undoubtedly, true, as it has been present in all ages since the fall of Adam. However, to attempt to use personal, identified ministries as examples of this occurrence is grossly judgemental, unbiblical and weakening to the body of Christ.

On the other hand, Seduction?? A Biblical Response takes us back into relevant Scripture passages that support the concepts under attack. This book presents us with a model for not only viewing these concepts as God-centered, but also for dealing with other concepts or lifestyles we may encounter.

When in doubt, believers need to go to the Word for truth. The Word separates as a two-edged sword; the Word also keeps God on the throne of our lives. God becomes our total source for tearing down the devil's strongholds that weaken our ministry.

I trust you will find the research, organization and focus of this book a valuable asset to your Christian growth. God bless you as you prayerfully study its messages.

Richard L. Watson
Dean of the Graduate School of Education
Oral Roberts University

THE HUNT'S ON

By Florence K. Biros / Son-Rise Publications

The Hunt's on. In fact, the Hunt has been on. For months Dave Hunt has nearly monopolized the Christian media. Magazines, TV, radio, newspapers and every form of communication have featured Mr. Hunt and his book — **The Seduction of Christianity.**

His claims concerning seduction have sent literally hundreds of thousands scurrying to bookstores. The results have been awesome. Churches (Evangelical and Charismatic alike) have lost numbers and many Christian ministries have felt pangs of suspicion and rejection because of people's paranoia. Pastors, theologians, Christian counselors with Spirit-filled messages have become victims of the Hunt. Out of fear, members of congregations have sent darts of accusation at stable men of God.

Having compiled the book **Expand Your Horizon** (which feaures two of the major targets of the **Seduction of Christianity** — Paul Yonggi Cho and Dr. Robert Schuller), I personally began to question what I had written there. Was I among the seduced? Were these two "giants" in the kingdom of the Christian world today truly of the occult? Was Dave Hunt's and T.A. McMahon's message of seduction totally right?

In order to answer my question, I felt it necessary to go on a hunt of my own. Immediately following my initial encounter with the **Seduction of Christianity,** I went to the ONLY SOURCE I know that has the absolute truth — God's Word!

Scripture after scripture told of positive mental attitude, visions and dreams, plus nearly every aspect of Christianity which Dave Hunt and T.A. McMahon have shot down in the pages of their book. In the midst of my search for truth, Dr. "Tommy" Reid, pastor of the Full Gospel Tabernacle in Buffalo, New York, sent me a copy of **Seduction?? A Biblical Response.** He and Mark Virkler (a theologian from the Buffalo School of the Bible) had put together an answer to the seduction question. Page after page of scriptures, and critiques by both Mark and Tommy gave answers that I had been seeking. As I read through the book, which was intended to be a study guide, I began to feel at peace. It had over eleven hundred scriptures to back its stand.

Yet, somehow I felt more should be added so that laymen everywhere could find the answers they were searching for. When Tommy Reid came to Youngstown, Ohio, for a speaking engagement, I had the opportunity to meet with him and discuss the need to expand the book and put it on the mass market. We decided that we should work toward that end.

After that it seemed as though the Lord took over. A friend of mine gave me a critique of Hunt and McMahon's book, written by Alan Langstaff of Eden Prairie, Minnesota, (the leader of Kairos Ministries). That same critique had appeared in Charisma Magazine. When I talked with Alan by phone, he said that he was going to debate Dave Hunt on

April 21 on a California radio network. He offered to let us use any of his material to expand the original version of **Seduction?? A Biblical Response** into a book that would satisfy everyone's need for answers.

Shortly after that I attended a FGBMFI rally in New Kensington, Pennsylvania, where I spoke briefly with Demos Shakarian about the project. Jim Tricco (a Full Gospel Businessman from Pittsburgh) suggested, "You ought to contact my pastor, Dr. Laine. Our church was in an uproar until he tore the book apart and answered each question biblically. We had a big meeting meant just for our congregation, but others came from the outside. After the pastor had explained the entire book — page-by-page — the results were unbelievable! At the end of the evening both sides felt satisfied. People from extreme points of view said that his explanation had satisfied them completely!"

Because of this Dr. James Laine became the target for the next part of my hunt. After listening to his tapes, I knew his critique should be included in the book. What he had to say made me realize that there are some things that should concern each of us:

1. Anything a Christian does should be Christ-centered. Jesus should be the nucleus of each of our lives.

2. Hunt and McMahon's writing about the **Seduction of Christianity** should make all of us aware of the possibility of seduction. We need to discern people and their ministries and seek the guidance of the Holy Spirit in our decisions. It is imperative that we seek answers directly from the Word of God. In this respect, Hunt and McMahon actually have done us a service.

3. We should be on guard that we are not carried away with one single facet of Christianity. In our lives we need balance in all things.

It is not the purpose of this book to seek vengeance or to shoot down the authors or the content of **The Seduction of Christianity.** This book is written out of concern:

1. for all of those Christians who have experienced inner turmoil, fear, confusion and doubt because of what has been said and written by the authors of **The Seduction of Christianity.**

2. for the controversy and division brought about within individual churches and within the Body of Christ by the authors and their book.

3. for those Christian leaders who have been wounded by statements and implications in the book and whose ministries have been adversely affected by reaction to the book and public statements made by the authors.

It is our prayer that the Holy Spirit, the Source of all truth from the Father and Son, will guide the readers of this response into peace and understanding through Him.

May your "hunt" lead you into all truth in JESUS!

INTRODUCTION

Rev. Thomas Reid

As the little commuter plane descended into the airport at Harrisburg, my heart literally "jumped" inside of me. I had been around the world, preached four successive services in the great church in Seoul, ministered to thousands of pastors at the leading conventions in our nation, but this trip was "special." Excitement about where I was going to preach tonight made me feel as if this was one of the most important occasions of my ministry.

Youthful Pastor Larry Kreider of Dove Fellowship met me as I came past the security gate. He looked younger than I had expected. I had heard so much about this fellowship that perhaps I expected an older man. His accomplishment was to build a church of over one thousand members, without a building. I had told thousands of pastors around the world that the church is people, not buildings, and believed that someday I would meet a man who would prove what I had said is true. Now for the first time I was sitting in a van beside the man who was my "personal hero."

I said, "Larry, I am thrilled to be with you; I am anxious to see your church." Larry shared with me his Mennonite background (I had always been impressed with the work of the Mennonite people), as well as his Charismatic experience. I knew I was about to see what I believed was perhaps the most biblical church structure in America, and I was really thrilled with that opportunity.

After dinner at a lovely restaurant, we drove to the church office, then eventually to a large converted barn where we were to meet with over 200 home group leaders of this large congregation. I began to realize that what I had heard about Dove Fellowship was really true. Here was a congregation of over 1,000 people that did not have a church building, but literally met in homes as did the church in Jerusalem. (Acts 20:20) They did come together on Sunday, using rented facilities in two locations throughout the city of Lancaster, but the church was literally like the early church, their "houses of worship" were the homes of the people.

I had always believed this was possible, but had never seen it actually work. More than 200 group leaders filled the seats in the barn and began to excitedly worship God; and when Larry introduced me to speak, I felt a prophetic anointing come over me. I shared what God had laid on my heart, and the meeting came to a conclusion.

After service, we went to one of Lancaster's Pennsylvania Dutch restaurants to eat. As we sat down, Larry and his associate handed me a book entitled **The Seduction of Christianity.** He said, "Have you seen this book?" and I answered that I had heard about it, but had not seen it, nor did I know exactly what it was about.

I quickly leafed through the book, and noted the names of many of my close personal friends, Dr. Paul Y. Cho, Dr. Kenneth Hagin, Bishop Earl

Paulk, and numerous other men I had come to love. I regarded most of these men among my closest and most esteemed friends and ministering Brethren. My mind went back to 1963 when Dr. Paul Cho was my interpreter, and along with my Father, we preached the first Revival in the new church he had founded in Seoul. It was a small church of about 600 members. God blessed in a marvelous way, and the young pastor traveled with me throughout Korea as an interpreter and co-evangelist. During this time a lifelong friendship developed between the two of us as young preachers.

I remembered having Dr. Cho invite my family back to Full Gospel Central Church, twenty years after leaving, for a "homecoming." Standing four separate times in the pulpit on that Sunday, preaching to over 120,000 people in one single Sunday is a memory I will always carry with me. But perhaps the single greatest memory is of that great preacher taking my little nine year old daughter, sitting with her on the grass, and treating her as if she were the most important person in the world.

I knew this man, I had studied his theology, heard him preach scores of times, as I have traveled with him around the world. I had spent much time in prayer with him, hundreds of hours of personal fellowship with him as a person, perhaps no American knew him better than I.

My eyes filled with tears as I read the unbridled attack against my friend.

Then I noted the name of Robert Schuller. How many times his messages had inspired me. At a time of my life when people across America were talking about my personal success, but I inwardly felt like "giving up the ministry," Dr. Schuller's ministry had not only encouraged my wife and me, but had given us a reason to "carry on."

I thought of the last dinner I had had in his home, of the times when we had discussed the orthodoxy of his theology. I remember reading his book, **Self Esteem, the New Reformation,** and how that book had affected not only my thinking, but my love for God as a Person.

One cannot know Robert Schuller without loving him. His warmth, his dedication to his wife and family, his desire to be biblical and scriptural in all that he believes, comes across strongly in every conversation I had had with him.

My closest friends! I screamed inside, how can anyone who loves the same God attack them like this?

Then I saw the name of Kenneth Hagin, and my memory went back to a little restaurant in Orlando, Florida, where I was with Brother and Sister Hagin until the early hours of the morning, hearing him share his experiences with the Lord. I remembered the first time I had heard him preach, and how I had marveled at his knowledge of the Word of God. I remembered his passionate love for God's Word; his strong desire to interpret it accurately was the obsession of his life.

Most of all, my friend Kenneth Hagin, was a man of prayer, a man of deep spiritual insight, and the man I had always regarded as the "person who walked closer to Jesus than any person I had ever met."

I remember turning to my associate, David Bemis, when I arose from the table that night and saying, "David, you have met the one man who knows Jesus better than perhaps any other person on earth." David turned to me, rather awe-stricken by the past few hours and obviously moved by what we had heard and seen in this private conversation, and nodded in the affirmative, perhaps too awe-stricken to speak in articulate words.

My heard cried, "Oh, if this man could only know my friend, Kenneth Hagin, and his love for God's Word, he would never write such things about God's servant."

Then I glanced further and the name of my very close personal brother in Christ, Earl Paulk, leaped off the page. Bishop Earl Paulk, Christian gentleman, lover of God's Word, extremely close friend, a man that had become as much like a brother to me as any man I had ever known.

If he could have only felt the presence of the Holy Spirit at Chapel Hill Harvester Church. If he could have only known the passion for orthodoxy that my friend Earl and I share together. Perhaps sometimes misunderstood by some, Earl Paulk has the greatest desire I have ever seen in any single man to "live out" and "fully understand" concepts and teaching of the Word of God.

My mind raced as I held the book in my hand. I read the name of Robert Tilton, again, my friend. I remember calling Bob to book Dr. Cho to speak in his church for the first time. I remember my wife and I, staying at the same motel in Winter Haven, Florida, with Bob, eating our meals together, during the first time we met face to face.

What a loving, kind brother Bob Tilton has always been to me. My mind flashed to the many "Tilton tapes" I had listened to, and the many times Bob had told me he had listened to my tapes. The one thing which always characterized a "Tilton tape" was my brother's love and constant quoting of God's Word. Being of Baptist background, this man had as great a respect for the Word as any man I have ever known. Sure, he preached success in life, but with a profusion of biblical truth to substantiate the position of Scripture concerning true biblical success.

By this time tears filled my eyes, my voice broke, and Larry said to me, "Tommy, what do you think about the book? My mind tore inner pain that I had never experienced before in my life. Someone had hurt my family, those I loved, those I believed in, those who are most of all my brothers in Christ.

I read down the list; every single person in the list was a personal friend. They lead the Body of Christ in America today. I felt as if they were the "Prophets" of this generation, and I wondered if the authors had ever tried to sit down and talk with my friends.

My mind raced to my own preaching. If these men are to be judged as non-orthodox, then he would judge me the same way. It is obvious that these men have become my friends because we agree in much of our theological interpretation of Scripture. I have preached strongly about positive mental attitude, the reformation of society by the church, the positive confession of the promises of the Word of God, and the use of God-inspired visions and dreams.

Perhaps if nothing else, we must develop a more defined theological position on these issues, in order to defend ourselves more fully. Then I wondered if "defense" is really proper; theological disputes are almost impossible to settle. Calvinists and Armenians will never fully settle their issue, for both feel they are right. Would we just involve ourselves in argument for argument's sake, and hang our "dirty wash" before the entire world to see?

As I slid the book back across the table to Larry and his associate, panic gripped me. I worried about all those people who could not properly define truth, who would read this book, and then becoming "judges" of truth in our church, and in every church where they attend. I wondered if we were headed toward another inquisiton. Were we Christians going to become more like the Scribes and Pharisees, and judge everyone by our own intellectual interpretation of Scripture? "Larry, I don't know," but I did know that thousands of people would be hurt, as I had been hurt.

Something happened inside of me that night. I think I felt like Christ felt when he prayed the prayer in John 17. He obviously wept for the divisions then in this body and for those yet to come in this body.

I hurt for my friends, I hurt most of all for my Lord and the divisions that have come in his Body.

I went to the motel that night and tossed and turned. What I had thought would be the most exciting day of my life turned out to be the day when my heart was broken for the broken Body of Christ.

I do not want these pages to be pages of defense of our theology. I do not want them to be pages of attack against my brother who wrote **The Seduction of Christianity.** I do not intend them to be a great theological discourse defending the theologies of the man I love in Christ. I do want them to be a message to the reader to honestly take the Scripture and examine for himself the purity of teaching of my brethren. Please do not judge them as others have done, by a few quotations taken out of context. Examine them as I have done, by what they preach in the full context in which they preach it, and by the way in which they live before God and man. May we always remember that it was Jesus who said, "By this shall all men know that YE and MY disciples, that ye have love one for another," and our master also said, "Judge not that ye be not judged."

TABLE OF CONTENTS

CRITIQUE OF
THE SEDUCTION OF CHRISTIANITY

Thomas F. Reid

A Christian leader recently said, "there is nothing more dangerous than religion in the hands of a negative person." Before any minister prepares a sermon, before any writer pens an article for a magazine, or any author begins a new manuscript for a book, those words should be placed prominently in front of his typewriter or desk. Those words should consistently shape the preparation of his sermons and any written material.

I have often reflected on preceeding generations of those who wielded the sword, or burned others at the stake because they felt their interpretation of Scripture was ultimate truth. With all of the negative magazine articles, books, and media presentations in which believers attack other believers, I wonder what physical reprisals we might inflict upon each other, if the law of the United States would permit.

The Seduction of Christianity is a book that I personally believe is doing more to divide the Body of Christ than any other single event of modern history. Perhaps my observations may seem extreme; however, let me share with you the reasons I feel so strongly.

First, the author is not an expression of a Berean mentality. A true Berean examines the Scripture to see whether a teaching is "so" according to the Scripture. David Hunt has chosen the very opposite approach, for he seeks to prove these things are "not so." The entire manuscript is an attempt to prove error rather than to prove truth.

Secondly, the author does not take into consideration the history of the Church. It is my own practice, after examining the Scripture to see if something is "so", to examine Church history, to see if the Church fathers interpret the Scripture in a similar manner. David Hunt does not seriously take Church history into consideration in his manuscript.

Thirdly, the author focuses on the beliefs of the cults, rather than on the teaching of Scripture. He compares the teachings of the Christian leaders of this day against what the cults believe. This is faulty reasoning in its highest form. Should one use this system of reasoning, one could take other statements of these leaders out of context, find them in disagreement with a cult, and thus "prove" they are orthodox. On the other hand, utilizing this form of reason, one could take the statements of a Mormon, or a Jehovah's Witness, compare it with a cult, and prove the Mormon or the Jehovah's Witness to be orthodox. Thus, the author establishes no standard with which to judge orthodoxy, since he uses the teaching of the cult, rather than the mutually agreed upon evangelical interpretation of Scripture, as a standard to judge the person's orthodoxy.

Fourthly, David Hunt fails to see that the presence of a counterfeit proves there is a real thing. There would be no reason for a printer to produce a counterfeit one-hundred-dollar bill if there were not a presence of the genuine one. One of his major approaches throughout the manuscript is to prove that the counterfeit believes in visions and dreams, that the counterfeit believes in influencing society, and that the counterfeit believes in man being indwelt by God, thus "proving" that any orthodox person who teaches such truths must be cultish. The VERY FACT THAT SOME CULTS TEACH SUCH THINGS (however perverted the teaching may be) simply means that there must be a genuine from which it was derived. The serious student studies the difference between the false and the real, but does not deny the existence for the real simply because there is a substitute.

I would add that the rainbow belonged to God's covenant long before there was a "New Age Theology." I refuse to give up divine truth, and divine symbolism to satanic forces, when they truly belong to the redeemed. I refuse to conclude that visions and dreams are the sole property of the cults, when I know they are rightfully the property of the Church. In EVERY generation God has spoken to his prophets through vision and dream. I refuse to give up my positive mental attitude in times of trial to those who use biblical teaching and adultrate it to their level. It is my property first, for I am a child of God. THE PRESENCE OF THE COUNTERFEIT ONLY PROVES THE EXISTENCE OF THE GENUINE.

Perhaps the most dangerous part of this book is the mutinous attacks upon orthodox Christian leadership. The men whose names are mentioned in this manuscript are not only men of God, but they are also men who adhere to orthodox Christianity.

Before we write articles or books which may serve to discredit a brother or sister in Christ, we need to determine the standard by which we judge orthodoxy. Therefore, the most significant question I can possibly ask is "WHAT IS THE BASIS FOR JUDGING ORTHODOXY?" Although you may judge orthodoxy more narrowly, I suggest two primary bases: (1) "Does that person believe in the diety, lordship, and sacrificial atonement of Jesus Christ?" and (2) "Does that person believe in the Nicene or Apostles' Creed?"

Perhaps the most penetrating question I would raise is:

WHAT IS GOD SAYING TO THE CHURCH TODAY?

Most Christian leaders agree that God is saying four major things to the church today:

1. THE NEED FOR REPENTANCE

2. PRAYER

3. THE NEED TO UNDERSTAND WHO WE ARE IN CHRIST

4. THE NEED TO EMBRACE A WORLD VIEW

Interestingly enough, it is in these four areas where David Hunt levels his greatest attack against church leadership. The men who have been specifically prophetic in calling the church to repentance, to prayer, to recognize their position in Christ, and to realize their responsibility to the world are the VERY PROPHETS whom David Hunt attacks.

In the remainder of this article, I would call your attention to what God is saying to the church today. I would remind you of the words of the Apostle: "Let him who has ears hear what the Spirit saith unto the churches."

REPENTANCE

There is no doubt in my mind that repentance is one of the areas that God is speaking to the Church today. Repentance was the theme of "Washington for Jesus," when over 700,000 people gathered in the mall in Washington to repent before God for the nation.

The Gospel accounts begin with the teaching of John the Baptist declaring "REPENT, FOR THE KINGDOM OF GOD or (THE REIGN OF GOD) IS AT HAND." When those who came for repentance asked him what they should repent of, he talked to them not of their ACTIONS or SINFUL ACTS, but rather of their NEGATIVE ATTITUDES. He taught that if a person had two coats, his attitude should be to enlarge his world by including another human being in a significant way. He talked about contentment with wages, not intimidating another person. Each time he dealt with ATTITUDES.

I believe that TRUE BIBLE REPENTANCE deals with ATTITUDES far more than ACTIONS. If a person has his attitudes cleansed, then he will not want to sin against himself or against his brother. True BIBLE repentance deals with our THINKING. That is why Jesus dealt not with the ACT of adultery, but rather with the THOUGHT of adultery. That is why Jesus dealt not with the ACT of murder, but rather with the ATTITUDE of hatred.

True repentance led the Apostle Paul to have an attitude in writing to the Philippians from prison which said, "When there is no purity around me, I think of those things that are PURE; when there is no JUSTICE around me, my thoughts are of things which are JUST; when there is nothing around me of GOOD REPORT, I think of those things of GOOD REPORT.

POSITIVE MENTAL ATTITUDE does not have its basis in the cult which began with Mr. Holmes, but rather in the deep-seated results of TRUE BIBLE REPENTANCE.

PRAYER

The second thing that God is saying to the Church is to call the Church to prayer. The APOSTLE OF PRAYER in this generation is Dr. Paul Y. Cho. Ten thousand people daily are in prayer at Dr. Cho's Prayer Mountain. No one in the history of the Church has led more people (and pastors) into a dynamic life of prayer than Dr. Cho. To attack his methodology of prayer as being unorthodox is, in my estimation, to STONE A PROPHET.

I would remind the reader, that seldom is God heard with an audible VOICE, but He often articulates His message in pictures, visions, or dreams, just as He did in both Old and New Testament times. To Abraham, Joseph, Ezekiel, Isaiah, and almost every other prophet, God spoke in both vision and dream. Jesus said "I DO ONLY THOSE THINGS I SEE THE FATHER DO." Peter changed the world with his dream in Acts 10, and John was enraptured into perhaps the greatest VISION of Church history, in the book of Revelation.

The human mind does not think in words, but rather in pictures. When we were children, our parents pointed to the picture of a car, or horse, or airplane, and we began to associate the WORD with the IMAGE or PICTURE. That is simply because GOD programmed the human mind to think in PICTURES. The language of the Holy Spirit is, according to Dr. Cho, the language of VISION AND DREAM.

I submit to you that GOD IS CALLING THE CHURCH TO PRAYER. When the Church learns to pray properly, it will learn the biblical use of VISION AND DREAM. VISUALIZATION is not the technique of Eastern mystics; it is intended by God to be the very medium of the communication of our FAITH to HIM, and HIS ideas to US.

Last of all, I would call your attention to the fact that Church history proves again and again the belief of the Church fathers in vision and dream. Let me refer to a few:

AUGUSTINE: Augustine took the entire Twelfth Book in **De Genesi ad Litteram** to explain his understanding of dreams and vision.

POLYCARP: He saw the pillow under his head catch fire and realized that this image of destruction signified his own impending capture and death.

JUSTIN MARTYR: He believed that dreams are sent by both evil spirits and God.

IRENAEUS: He explained that although God is Himself invisible to the eye directly, He gives us visions and dreams through which He conveys the likeness of His nature and His glory.

TERTULLIAN: "And thus we - who both acknowledge and reverence, even as we do the prophecies, modern visions as equally promised to us, and consider the other powers of the Holy Spirit as an agency of the Church for which also He was sent, administering all gifts in all, even as the Lord distributed to every one . . ."

CONSTANTINE: Lactantius writes of the heavenly vision that gave Constantine his great victory in 300 A.D.

A VIEW OF OUR POSITION IN CHRIST

I believe perhaps the greatest revelation of the Holy Spirit to the Church today is WHO WE ARE IN CHRIST.

Until we truly learn that WE ARE THE ONGOING INCARNATION, and until we learn our UNION WITH HIM, AND HIS UNION WITH US, we cannot fully comprehend the truth of Christianity.

CHRIST IN US, THE HOPE OF GLORY, and, IT IS NOT I THAT LIVE, BUT CHRIST THAT LIVETH IN ME, are but a small sample of the multitude of proof text scriptures which deal with the subject. The very promise of the New Covenant was that He would write His LAW in our HEARTS.

It is this very TRUTH that God has so aptly spoken through such men as E.W. Kenyon, Kenneth Hagin, Kenneth Copeland, Jerry Sevelle, Robert Schuller, and many others. Not a new truth, but the very basis of New Testament Christianity. Although we need to be warned of potential extremes, let us not lose sight of this MOST VITAL TRUTH OF OUR CHRISTIAN FAITH.

A NEW WORLD VIEW

David Hunt's last attack was against those who are building a biblical basis for the reformation of society.

We are replete with evangelical Christian leaders who are making a difference in their world today. Jerry Fallwell, with his Moral Majority, and David Wilkerson, in the rehabilitation of drug addicts through his Teen Challenge, are prime examples of the Evangelical being involved in his world.

Of necessity, we must develop a theology of responsibility. We will not work for the transformation of our society if we believe that society cannot be transformed.

David Chilton states in his book, PARADISE RESTORED, "The whole rise of Western civilization — science and medicine, the arts, constitutionalism, the jury system, free enterprise, literacy, increasing productivity, a rising standard of living, the high status of women, IS ATTRIBUTABLE TO ONE MAJOR FACT: THE WEST HAS BEEN TRANSFORMED BY CHRISTIANITY.

I would remind Mr. Hunt of the words of the famed hymn:

JESUS SHALL REIGN WHERE ERE THE SUN DOETH HIS SUCCESSIVE JOURNEYS RUN.

or the famed Christmas carol we all sing:

NO MORE LET SINS AND SORROWS GROW,
NOR THORNS INFEST THE GROUND.
HE COMES TO MAKE HIS BLESSINGS FLOW
FAR AS THE CURSE IS FOUND.

HE RULES THE WORLD
WITH GRACE AND TRUTH
AND MAKES THE NATIONS PROVE
THE GLORIES OF HIS RIGHTEOUSNESS
AND THE WONDERS OF HIS LOVE.

I submit to the reader that it has always been orthodox for the Christian Church to believe in changing or influencing its world for good. Surely God would have us preach the reformation of sociological structure through the teaching of the Lordship of Jesus Christ.

Let us be true Christian leaders by accepting our orthodox brother, even though we disagree with his emphasis in one area or another. I would conclude that Christianity is not being seduced by Dr. Cho, Dr. Schuller, or Rev. Bob Tilton. To the contrary, it is through such men that the Church is hearing what God is speaking in this day. We must take great care, or we, like the Pharisees of Jesus' day, will hold on to our TRADITIONS and fail to recognize what the Spirit is saying to the Church today.

A REPLY TO THE SEDUCTION OF CHRISTIANITY

By Alan Langstaff, Kairos Ministries Inc.
P.O. Box 27186, Golden Valley, MN 55427
(612)446-1721

Alan Langstaff debated David Hunt on California radio following the printing of this critique in **Charisma Magazine,** *190 N. Westmonte Drive, Altamonte Springs, Florida 32714. Copyright 1986, Strang Communications Company. Updated version as of May 1986 is as follows.*

It was the receptionist at our church who first asked me if I had read the book *THE SEDUCTION OF CHRISTIANITY.* It had been given to her by a member of her family who questioned the authority of her charismatic experience and beliefs. From then on I noticed it cropping up in all sorts of conversations, with ministers and lay people alike. All of them asked me the same questions: "What do you think of this book? If the authors are right, are we wrong about so many things we thought were right?"

On my way to minister in Winnipeg, Canada, I stopped for a lunch break in Thief River Falls, where I noticed the book prominently displayed in the window of a Christian bookshop, so I bought it and read it. What do I think about it now? Quite honestly, I believe it is *a very dangerous book* that will do much harm and *be used* greatly to undermine the faith of many who find the argument presented persuasive. For this reason I am writing this critique to examine the issues more clearly. As I said, it is a very dangerous book, *not* becuase it is all wrong in what it says — it is *not.* In fact, if it were, no answer would be required — the errors would be evident to the readers. Rather, it is dangerous because it is *such a persuasive mixture of truth and error that the average reader finds himself caught up in an avalanche of quotations and so-called research that it is well-nigh impossible for him to sort it all out.* In actual fact, the book lives up to its title, *SEDUCTION OF CHRISTIANITY.* It is itself seductive, for the style and approach of the authors serves to confuse the reader to the point that he accepts wrong conclusions

A brief overview of the book may be in order for those who have not read the book. (I do not recommend reading it, unless you are in a position of pastoral responsibility and need to have first-hand knowledge so as to be able to counsel people regarding the errors in the book.) It is concerned with the so-called seduction of Christianity in the last days through the latest "fashionable philosophies, including the danger in the growing acceptance and practice of positive and possibility thinking, healing of memories, self philosophies, holistic medicine." They name names — just about everyone is castigated, including Robert Schuller, Paul Yonggi Cho,

Charles Capps, Norman Vincent Peale, Agnes Sanford, Bruce Larson, Norman Grubb, Kenneth Copeland, Robert Tilton, Gloria Copeland, Ralph Wilkerson, John and Paula Sandford, Richard Foster, Robert L. Wise, Morton Kelsey, C.S. Lovett, Rita Bennett, Dennis and Matthew Linn, Ruth Carter Stapleton, Frank Laubach, John Wimber, Earl Paulk, Francis MacNutt, Zig Ziglar, and others.

The heart of this message is simply this: The authors claim Christianity is being seduced through inroads of psychology into the church. Since they believe that psychology had is origins in the occult, they do not recognize the validity of **Christian** psychology. They believe there are three main "occult" techniques that are being used to seduce Christianity today (see page 157):

1) The power of thinking (positive mental attitude)
2) The power of speaking (positive confession)
3) Visualization

Hence, those who use any of these techniques are, by the authors' definition, promulgating occult teaching and satanic techniques.

Now please note carefully, Hunt and McMahon are *not* seeking to correct excesses and extremes in these teachings or to bring about a more balanced presentation regarding these matters. They are categorically claiming that the use of these three techniques is satanic. On page 158 they state, "The Bible does not teach such methods." They take an all-or-nothing approach and in their view, these techniques are all wrong — they are occult techniques.

But are they? Let's examine the issue carefully. Let's start with a **basic question.** How do you test the theories of a book like this? I would suggest, that when you seek to investigate a subject there are four steps you must take. These four steps are:

1) **RESEARCH**
   You *read* and *study* all the material that you can on the subject. This includes *observing* at first hand the things you are studying, *reviewing* the books written by the men you are critiquing and *interviewing* them in person whenever possible, and personally *observing* the fruit of their ministry. (See Matthew 7:16).

2) **ANALYSIS**
   Once you have done your research, the next step is to analyze the information you have gathered. You must use a sound form of analysis, since research alone does not guarantee the correct conclusion. (See I Thessalonians 5:21).

3) PRESUPPOSITIONS

The methods you use for your analysis will be determined by certain presuppositions, namely, your convictions about what is true and what is not. Your analysis will always be colored and affected by the presuppositions with which you start. (See II Timothy 3:14).

4) CONCLUSIONS

Finally, all this leads you to your conclusions — the end product of the investigation. (See Acts 17:11).

Having studied the book, having listened on tape to David Hunt, the main author, and having engaged with him in a dialogue on the book on live radio, it is my opinion that the basic conclusions of the book are false, having been reached through:
a)   Inadequate research
b)   Incorrect analysis, and
c)   Faulty presuppositions

Look at these one by one:

1) INADEQUATE RESEARCH

It is my considered opinion that the authors do not demonstrate adequate research in three main areas.

First, it may come as a surprise to many readers to discover that, with the exception of Richard Foster, the authors did not contact any of the people that they critiqued in the book. Consequently, many feel that the authors have not done justice to these people, since they have failed to present a balanced view of their teaching and their ministry, and have sensationalized aspects of their teaching. Let us give a specific example. On pages 74-76 the authors deal with the ministry of John Wimber, but nowhere do they summarize his teaching. In actual fact, the main complaint against him seems to be that he recommended certain writers whom they consider to be satanically deceived. This is nothing less than "guilt by association." Likewise in their treatment of Dr. Cho, they make no study of his teaching and practice on prayer, which is the basis of all his ministry. Consequently, they do not seem to perceive the difference between visions that come from the carnal mind (or even from satanic origins) and those that are inspired by the Holy Spirit.

Matthew 18 lays down the procedures for dealing with a brother whom you consider to be in error. These procedures were not followed. The question is not whether those who were criticized would have given time to speak with the authors; the question is whether they ever tried.

Second, although the book gives the appearance of much research, often the quotes are taken out of context and used in such a way as to present a misleading impression. As an example, on page 49, squeezed in between two contemporary references, is an official United States statement which supposedly supports one world government, giving the impression that his is the policy of the present U.S. government. When you check the footnotes in the back of the book, you discover that the statement was made in 1964, 22 years ago, and has no validity today.

Thirdly, and of prime importance, there is a lack of biblical research. Subjects are raised with no attempt made to investigate the relevant teaching in Scripture on these subjects. (More about this later under the following heading.)

2) INCORRECT ANALYSIS

Although on a number of occasions the authors make references to the Berean principle found in Acts 17, (see page 224), they consistently fail to take their own advice.

First, unlike the Bereans they take what is written and compare it against occult teaching. But this is not the way to do it. Such an approach easily leads to the faulty conclusion that since there are similarities between the two, the writing must be satanic.

You test a man's teaching against Scripture, not against occult writers.

Second, unlike the Bereans, Hunt and McMahon do not go on the Scriptures to seek out what the Word says about a particular issue. In actual fact, they usually completely ignore what the Bible has to say. Maybe the reason is because they appear not so much to be investigating or analyzing a subject but rather proving what they already believe. Take as an example the question of "positive confession". They critique many of the writers on this issue, claiming that the belief that there is power in what you say is purely satanic. But a detailed study of Scripture will show that from Genesis ("then God said. . .") to the book of Revelation ("and they overcame him by the blood of the Lamb and the word of their testimony"), the Bible is full of references to the power of a positive confession.

Incidentally, Dave Hunt makes the charge that things like positive confession, positive mental attitude and inner healing are not biblical because you cannot find those words or phrases in Scripture. The *words* may not be there, but the *concepts* are. As an example, you cannot find the word "trinity" in the Bible, but the concept of a triune God is there.

A study of biblical passages such as Mark 11:23 ("whosoever shall *say* to this mountain. . ."), Romans 10:9 ("Confess with your mouth"), Acts 3:6, 7 ("in the name of Jesus Christ of Nazareth, walk") will show you that there is power in what you say, when it is spoken in faith under the anointing of the Holy Spirit in accordance with the Word of God.

Taken to its extreme, this erroneous view negating the power of the spoken word undermines all spoken ministries including preaching, healing, prayer, deliverance, prophecy and evangelism.

Third, there is a lack of understanding of cultural differences that affect the way people think and view reality. Western man from the Renaissance onward has been increasingly cast in the rational mold of logical, analytical thinking, but the Eastern mindset is quite different. Eastern man thinks more in terms of pictures, types and symbols. In the preface to his book, *PROFILES OF A LEADER,* Judson Cornwall points out that "the Bible is full of picture language. A-bounds in parables, similies, illustrations, comparisons and analogies, for the Holy Spirit understands the power of the anecdote or an analogy." Hence, a concept like visualization (which, like anything else, can be misused) is quite natural to the eastern mind and often quite foreign to the western mind. The Bible is cast in this Eastern thought form and even much of the prophecy in books like Daniel, Ezekiel and Revelation is of this kind. So, in actual fact, visualization (if that is the word you want to use) is quite biblical in concept. The key, however, is the *source* of it. If it comes from God and is inspired by the Holy Spirit, it is a legitimate aid to faith. If it comes out of the soul of man or, worse still, from occult sources, it is not. This is where discernment of spirits is needed.

3) FAULTY PRESUPPOSITIONS

Let us turn now to the presuppostions of the book. *"What are the premises upon which the authors build their thesis?"* Since nowhere in the book do they articulate clearly their own theological presuppositions, a little bit of detective work is required to begin to put them together.

Eventually, we discover that they hold a fundamentalist theological position. (See chapter 14). In particular, their spirituality is one that emphasizes transcendence of God and the low position of man as sinner in the sight of his creative God. This is a particular form of traditional evangelical spirituality. On page 104 they sum it up this way: "But the transcendant God of the Bible can reach in from outside, effecting His miracles. These include the whole range of triumph over natural law, but the most important miracles are forgiveness of sin, redemption, resurrection and the creation of new creatures for a new universe that He will someday bring into existence for the redeemed to inhabit. Having given us the power of choice so that we could freely choose to respond to his love, He will not violate our wills, and unlike the bargaining and appeasing involved with pagan gods, *our approach to the God of the Bible must be as unworthy sinners relying upon His grace and mercy, recognizing that there are no formulas that we can think or speak that will require Him to respond to us in a certain way."* (Emphasis mine!) Subsequent to writing this critique I contacted the publishers and was informed that Dave Hunt's church background is Plymouth Brethren, *i.e.* fundamentalist.

The main author, David Hunt, was baptized in the Spirit around 1974 (see his book, *CONFESSION OF A HERETIC*) and states that he believes in miracles and healing. However, the issue is not what he has experienced in the past or what he believes. *The issue is* — what do the authors write in the book? The book does not present a typical charismatic or pentecostal theological position; rather, it presents typical fundamentalist theology, over - emphasizing the sovereignty of God at the expense of the exercise of man's will and faith. Consequently, there are virtually no positive references in the book to the gifts of the Spirit, tongues, or miracles (except under the initiative of a sovereign God).

For further evidence of the author's ultra-extreme position on the sovereignty of God, see pages 100 and 101, especially the following quote: "In contrast to the biblical doctrine of grace, this insistence that God Himself must work even His own miracles within a framework of laws that enable us to tap into and dispense power by what we think, speak, or do is the basis for all ritualism and occultism." On the basis of that definition, you virtually end up in a form of predestination, because it rules out even the law of sin and death and salvation. (Incidentally, to be consistent, the authors should have included Bill Bright in the list of people under attack with his promotion of the "Four Spiritual Laws". Do you see how ridiculous this position becomes? Also, what about Bill Gothard who teaches about visualization?)

Note, also, the statement on page 101: "There is no cause-and-effect relationship between man and spirits, whether angels or demons, any more than between man and God; evil spirits encourage this idea in order to deceive and enslave. We must never forget that our *only* approach to God is as unworthy sinners relying upon His grace and love. Whatever is governed by 'law' to which even God is subject is the basis of all ritual and occultism."

That is not a scriptural understanding of the position that we have as believers. Whether you call it a law, or a principle, or a promise, God's Word makes is clear that God has made certain commitments to His people. If we do this, He will do that. (See for example, II Chronicles 7:14, the prayer for revival). Likewise, the promise of salvation as in Acts 2:37, 38; Acts 16:30, 31). *Without the assurance that God will remain true to His Word, we have no basis for trusting Him for anything.* Yes, it is on the basis of grace, but, that grace is extended to us in specific promises given to us in His Word — that's the basis of all believing prayer, positive confession and faith.

4) WRONG CONCLUSIONS

Therefore, because of inadequate research, incorrect analysis, and faulty presuppositions, the authors reach the erroneous conclusions that a positive mental attitude, positive confession and visualization are all satanic in origin.

But then you ask, "What about all the similarities that the authors show between current Christian teaching and practices and occult activities?" The reason for this similarity is *that the occult is a demonic attempt by Satan to counterfeit the real manifestation of the Spirit.* Hunt and McMahon refer to this explanation on page 140 but refute it.

If you and I were to counterfeit dollar bills we would not print a $9 note or an $11 note. No, we would try to counterfeit a $10 note that looked as close to the real thing as we could possibly make it. And that is what the devil is trying to do.

Take one biblical example from Acts, chapter 16. Here Paul comes in contact with the slave girl who "having a spirit of divination was bringing her masters much profit from fortune telling (vs. 16)." Her counterfeit occult gifts were very similar in practice to the operation of the true spiritual gifts of I Corinthians, chapter 12. For many days she followed Paul prophesying, "These men are bond servants of the Most High God who are proclaiming to you the way of salvation." After a number of days (presumably waiting to be sure), Paul exorcised the spirit of divination from the girl, and she was set free. Interestingly enough, not one word she said was wrong. Her prophesying was a counterfeit expression of a spiritual gift, which was very similar to the real thing. The difference was the *source* — it came from the devil. True spiritual gifts come from the Holy Spirit. Much that is happening today is of the same nature, for we are involved in a worldwide outpouring of the Holy Spirit, accompanied by signs, wonders and miracles and also a revival of occult practices that often counterfeit the real thing.

That is why, like Paul, we need to be able to rightly discern the real from the counterfeit, to separate that which is of the Holy Spirit from that which is of the occult.

WHAT CAN WE LEARN FROM THE BOOK?

I said at the beginning that the book is a mixture of truth and error. The authors throw out the baby with the bath water, but nonetheless, they do put a finger on some issues that need to be looked at. So there are some things we can learn:

1)   Charismatics are often too gullible and accept anything. There are extreme and even wrong teachings as well as a lack of balance in some of the teachers in charismatic circles today. We need to heed the words of Proverbs 14:15, "The naive believes everything but the prudent man considers his steps."

2)   Second, we need to recognize the ever-present danger of beginning in the Spirit and slipping over the line into the flesh (or as Watchman Nee calls it. . ."the latent power of the soul") and into the occult. Not all the PMA teaching today is biblical in content and Holy Spirit in origin. Often it can be more soulish than spiritual.

3)   There needs to be a more thorough examination of the whole area of "inner healing" which in particular seems open to abuse more than many other areas of ministry. Its practices need to be studied more diligently in the light of Scripture for there is too much of a mixture of psychological techniques in with the biblical teaching. This is not a challenge to the validity of this kind of ministry, but a plea for more discernment regarding the practice of the same.

One last word, especially to pastoral leaders. In seeking to help people work through the issues that this book raises, a couple of practical points:

a)   Don't try to defend everything and everyone's ministry and reject everything that the authors are saying as being not true. Remember it's a mixture of truth and error.

b)   Go for the major issues that are the *foundation* for the *investigation.* That is the key to it all.

c)   Don't get involved in endless argument — that is precisely what the devil wants you to do. It will only breed confusion and doubt and undermine people's faith.

d)   Get on with the job of the ministry that God has given to you and your people. Let's see more miracles, signs and wonders and a positive affirmation of who we are *in Him.*

CRITIQUE OF
THE SEDUCTION OF CHRISTIANITY

By James A. Laine

Rev. James A. Laine is pastor of Faith Community World Outreach Center in Bethel Park, Pennsylvania, and was former co-host with Russ Bixler on a talk show over Channel 40, the Christian Cornerstone Network out of Wall, Pennsylvania. Deeply concerned over the growing confusion and negative effects produced by the book **The Seduction of Christianity,** he felt the necessity to speak to his congregation regarding the controversial questions which had arisen. The following is written from his message to his congregation. His opening prayer was: "Father, we ask that YOU would cause us to glorify Jesus' name in everything we meditate upon and everything we do and say concerning this book. We ask, Father, that You would direct us so that our whole purpose would be to exalt Him and to stand for Your Word. And, Lord, in Jesus' name, we commit this matter of concern to Your care, asking for Your grace, Your counsel, Your love, and Your peace. In Jesus' name, Amen."

We need to understand that when God moves in the body of Christ to bring about a deeper understanding of a biblical truth, this truth always moves to an extreme position. This is known as the pendulum effect. Throughout Church history, this effect can be seen repeatedly. Time and time and again, the pendulum has swung widely in the history of the Full Gospel Movement. When God began to reveal the truth regarding deliverance, suddenly everyone was delivering everything all the time, seeing demons behind every bush and believing every Christian needed deliverance.

When God began to open our understanding regarding the submission of wives, suddenly wives were to submit everything, including beatings and taking part in robbing banks. Everyone went to the extreme with this truth.

When we received the authority message, we moved into the extreme of shepherding. Currently, we see the pendulum swinging in the messages of prosperity and faith. Regardless of what truth God begins to reveal to us more deeply, we take it to the extreme.

Those who teach these messages occasionally may take them to the extreme. However, even when the teachers present a balanced truth, those who hear frequently apply the message in an unbalanced fashion. It is God's desire that we walk right down the middle of a truth. Given time to go through the process of experiencing opposite ends of a truth, the Church usually finds the middle.

The book **The Seduction of Christianity,** by David Hunt and T.A. McMahon, is an attempt by the authors to correct an extreme; their correction, however, is in itself an extreme. The book is obviously a controversial writing. It does contain truth, but it cannot be read as one would read the Bible, which is all truth and can therefore be received as it is. **The Seduction of Christianity** cannot be read in this manner; it must be carefully examined in order to distinguish between truth and error.

Whenever we read a controversial writing, we need to realize that there is an issue involved about which the author has strong opinions, which may be reflected in an extreme position. We are likely to find such words and phrases as "every," "all", "surely everyone knows." These need to be examined — perhaps everyone doesn't know! You will notice "if then" clauses, leading you to believe that, "If this is true, then this is true." All of these logic statements need to be carefully checked.

An author who pursues an extreme viewpoint is likely to overstate his case through exaggeration, thus negating what he is trying to say. If he believes someone is teaching an error, he will, at the expense of accuracy, quote only the most "damning" words, phrases, and thoughts from that teacher. Removed from their context, quotations may very well distort what the person is actually teaching. Unless you are familiar with all the writings to which Hunt and McMahon refer, you may not know whether what you are reading is a fair and true representation of the teaching of these people.

You also must keep in mind the fact that an author frequently outgrows his early writing. A particular piece may not be reflective of anything else he has ever written. He may even regret having written it, but once in print, it cannot be recalled.

Another highly damaging technique used by Hunt and McMahon requires that the reader use caution in order to avoid being drawn onto erroneous conclusions. They frequently refer to a known occultist and then, without any transition, mention the writings or teachings of a Christian. The reader is then drawn into believing the occultist and the Christian are teaching the same thing.

Hunt and McMahon say that we should examine those whom they criticize on the basis of the Word and the fruit of their ministry, and yet their book does not take this approach. The approach used by the authors is reflective of their background in researching the occult and the New Age. Seeing similar things in the occult, the New Age movement, and Christianity, they reach the conclusion that the occult and the New Age have entered into the Church. What we may see or not see in the occult cannot be the basis for judging what we see in the Church. Even as the authors have said (not done), we must use the standard of the Word of God.

There are two kingdoms — the Kingdom of God, and the kingdom of satan. Everything in God's kingdom is positive — everything in satan's kingdom is negative. Everything in God's kingdom is real — everything is satan's kingdom is a counterfeit of that which is real. Satan has a counterfeit for everything we have in the Kingdom of God.

Those in God's kindom operate by faith, word, and spirit — those in satan's kingdom operate by fear. Those in God's kingdom operate in love — those in satan's kingdom operate by lust (they call it "love," but it is lust). Those in the Kingdom of God worship and pray — those in satan's kingdom worship and pray. There is healing and prosperity in God's kingdom — there is healing and prosperity in satan's kingdom. It would be absurd for us to observe a church involved in prayer, worship, and healing and say, "Those people pray, they are being healed — there must be something occult about this church!"

This is the type of thing Hunt and McMahon do repeatedly in their book. They have seen it in the occult, they have seen it in the New Age movement — and so they say, "If it is seen in the Body of Christ, it is wrong, because it is also found in the kingdom of satan!" This is a very bad assumption. The only standard by which we can judge is the same one the authors advocate — the Word of God. Do we see it in the Word? Is it scriptural, or is it not scriptural? If it is not acceptable within the teaching of the Word, we must not accept it. If it is acceptable within the teaching of the Word, then we will accept it.

Arguments from biblical silence are unreliable, at best, since anything can be argued from biblical silence. "The Word doesn't say we should drive cars; therefore, we should not drive cars." Yet, Hunt and McMahon frequently use such arguments when they use the phrase, "The Word doesn't say. . ." This approach can be carried to any extreme. An argument from biblical silence, whether for or against a position, is not a convincing one.

The authors spend considerable time saying that God is not a God of laws, that you cannot depend on laws in the Kingdom, and yet He is a God of law. He does everything according to principles He has established. He gave us law in the Old Testament because He is a God of law. He established laws which govern the functioning of the universe. The law of gravity affects all of us.

Everything has a pattern. Everything has a principle. Everything operates under laws. When we come against this concept and say that God is not a God of law — that we cannot depend on laws in His Word — we deny the nature of God at its very basis. He has revealed Himself as a God of law.

The Seduction of Christianity has created paranoia. It has caused many to be afraid of the abundant life in Jesus Christ — the life that Jesus has presented to us. It has made us afraid of certain words. If we hear anyone say "prosperity," or "healing," or "meditation," or "visualization," some of us immediately begin to think negative thoughts. We become fearful and suspicious of what is going on. The results have been disastrous. I have talked with some pastors who are receiving anonymous letters, phone calls, and face-to-face confrontations from their people every time they use such words. They are being bombarded every time they use the word "prosperity," or the phrase, "positive mental attitude."

Many pastors are being unjustly accused. For example, a pastor in Pittsburgh used the words "faith" and "prosperity" in a couple of his sermons and lost people from his congregation because of it. They had read the book! And yet, this man could not be termed a "faith" pastor. He is definitely not in that camp.

In our own congregation, we had people in counseling with a Spirit-filled Christian psychologist. They were doing very well under his care and ministry. Then some people read **The Seduction of Christianity**, and warned them, "You better get away from him! He is into the New Age! He is a psychologist! He is dangerous! You can't believe what he says." As a result, many removed themselves from his care. They have been damaged because of it. Many grave responses such as this have come from the book. This is why we need to use discernment concerning it and find out how we ought to respond to it. We ought to respond with discernment, rather than paranoia. Let us discern what is truth and what is error. Let us really look for the error and not get paranoid so that we find error everywhere. We need to search out error and remove it, rather than find error in everything.

THE NEW AGE

Hunt and McMahon, on page seven, define the New Age movement as "a broad coalition of networking groups all working for world religious experiences and beliefs that have their root in Eastern mysticism." They claim that the movement is firmly entrenched in the Church through such things as psychotherapy, visualization, meditation, bio-feedback, possibility thinking, holistic medicine and the entire spectrum of self-improvement and success motivation teachings.

MEDITATION

The Scripture says that we are to meditate. There is absolutely nothing wrong with meditation in a Christian context. The book says that meditation is part of the New Age movement but does not define it, and this lack causes a problem. New Age meditation is a counterfeit — Christian meditation is God's will.

POSITIVE CONFESSION

Positive confession is biblical. The Psalms are full of positive confession. What I teach at our Center is what I call 'positive confession.'

Positive biblical confession is a confession found often in the Psalms:

"My tears drench my pillow every night, my bones are withering away within me. I am being beseiged on every side. BUT THOU, O LORD, WILL DELIVER." These verses make up a statement of reality concerning the problems we face, but they include (here in caps) a positive confession that GOD is going to overcome the situation — that GOD is going to make the difference. That is positive biblical confession straight from God's Word! Check the Psalms for yourself. You will find many such examples.

HOLISTIC MEDICINE

Holistic medicine is another problematic area. There are holistic counselors who are totally into the New Age. If you go to a holistic doctor, and there is New Age literature in his office, you don't have to guess where he is coming from. Such New Age counselors and doctors are all over the nation! Holistic healers!

Yet, we also have born-again, Spirit-filled physicians who call themselves "holistic" healers and who are presenting Jesus, encouraging their patients to be born again, and telling them that Jesus Christ heals. They lay hands on them and pray for them to be healed. Their understanding of holistic healing is "ministry to the body, mind, and spirit."

In our ministry, we believe in treating the whole person by counseling the soul, by having a medical doctor prescribe medication or perform surgery, if needed, and by laying on of hands with prayer for spiritual healing. We recognize God as the Divine Healer, and the avenue for healing is His choice! Our constant prayer is that we be open to His leading.

So, you cannot say *carte blanche* that anyone who says he is involved in holistic medicine is New Age or occult! There are some very fine brothers and sisters out there who are calling their practice Christian "holistic medicine." These people are truly serving God, and you will have to use discernment, rather than write off all of those who are using holistic medicine as New Age or occult.

POSSIBILITY THINKING

If as a Christian you don't have possibility thinking, you don't have anything. God said to the Israelites, "I'm going to take you to the Promised Land." Without possibility thinking, there was no way for them to enter into the land of promise. What happened? They died in the wilderness because they didn't have any possibility thinking. They said, "We can't do it."

Some of the teaching regarding possibility thinking does contain error, but possibility thinking is found throughout the Body of Christ. It is a biblical principle, which, like all others, is indispensable.

SUCCESS AND MOTIVATIONAL TEACHING

The Bible is absolutely full of self-improvement and motivational teaching. It is the original motivational guide. It has motivated me to a changed life and has made me a new person. It has given me vision, it has given me goals, it has given me desires, plans, and purposes. Again, you cannot throw out all self-improvement and success motivation techniques!

Hunt and McMahon's statement that the New Age is firmly entrenched in the Church immediately causes division in the Body of Christ. They have come against the things of the Lord because they have seen the counterfeits of these things happening in the New Age movement. They lead us to believe that when we see words like "prosperity," "holistic medicine," "positive confession," or "possibility thinking," or "motivational thinking" being used within the Body of Christ, we are being invaded by the occult.

Hunt and McMahon, on page 12, give their definition of sorcery, which, in essence, states that any attempt to manipulate reality (inside, outside, past, present, or future) by different mind-over-matter techniques that run the gamut from alchemy and astrology to positive possibility thinking is sorcery. What does God tell us to do? "When you come up against the enemy and you see that they are greater and mightier than you, do not fear. I will deliver you. I will give you the victory. Have faith and trust in Me. I am God — I will do it." This is the essence of what He says to us time and time again. If that isn't possibility thinking, I don't know what is!

To call positive possibility thinking "sorcery" is to stand against truth. Such statements put people on the defensive when, biblically, they should be secure. We need to discern the difference between Bible-based possibility thinking and occult possibility thinking!

We reiterate: just because the occult uses something does not mean that the Church should stop using it. Again we stress that there are many things done in the occult which are similar to things within our Christian heritage. They have crosses, they draw much attention to blood, they pray, the worship, among other things. Does that mean we shouldn't?

SELF-IMAGE

On page 14, Hunt and McMahon write that "humility is out and self-esteem is in. . .," even though Scripture says, "Let each esteem others better than ourselves (Phil. 2:3 KJV)." They state that "it used to be common knowledge that the besetting sin of the human race was pride. Now, however, we are being told that our problem is not that we think too highly of ourselves, but too lowly, that we have a bad self-image, that our greatest need is to build up our self-esteem." This theme is also dealt with on pages 195 and 198 and other places throughout the book. Their basic premise is that there is no such thing as a poor self-image.

The authors say that in God's Word you never read of a prophet or a priest or a counselor dealing with a poor self-image — they are wrong! The Bible definitely speaks of a poor self-image. In I Samuel 9:2, we read, "And he had a son, whose name was Saul, a choice young man, and a goodly: and there was not among the children of Israel a goodlier person than he: from his shoulders and upward he was higher than any of the people." This was written before Saul was king. Saul was a beautiful specimen of humanity, taller than everybody else in Israel. He did not have to deal with the problem of being short — he was tall and goodlooking.

In Chapter 15 we learn that he was made king and was then told to go and wipe out the Amalekites, to destroy them and take no booty. In the seventeenth verse, he was rebuked because he had disobeyed:

17 And Samuel said, "Is it not true, though you were little in your own eyes, you were made the head of the tribes of Israel? And the Lord anointed you king over Israel.

18 And the Lord sent you on a mission, and said, 'Go and utterly destroy the sinners, the Amalekites, and fight against them until they are exterminated.'

19 "Why then did you not obey the voice of the Lord, but rushed upon the spoil and did what was evil in the sight of the Lord?"

20 Then Saul said to Samuel, "I did obey the voice of the Lord, and went on the mission on which the Lord sent me, and have utterly destroyed the Amalekites.

21 "But the people took some of the spoil, sheep and oxen, the choicest of the things devoted to destruction, to sacrifice to the Lord your God at Gilgal."

22 And Samuel said, "Has the Lord as much delight in burnt offerings and sacrifices us in obeying the voice of the Lord? Behold, to obey is better than sacrifice, And to heed than the fat of rams.

23 "For rebellion is as the sin of divination, And insubordination is as iniquity and idolatry. Because you have rejected the word of the Lord, He has also rejected you from being king."

24 Then Saul said to Samuel, "I have sinned; I have indeed transgressed the command of the Lord and your words, because I feared the people and listened to their voice.

25 "Now therefore, please pardon my sin and return with me, that I may worship the Lord."

26 But Samuel said to Saul, "I will not return with you; for you have rejected the word of the Lord, and the Lord has rejected you from being king over Israel."

Saul had a poor self image. He was "little in his own eyes." He was afraid of his people, so he listened to them, rather than God. Why he sinned is very clear — he had a poor self-image — and God judged him for that. He held that poor self-image against Saul and judged him because he acted out of it, rather than out of obedience to God.

Now we are being told that dealing with a poor self-image is witchcraft. When God judges a poor self-image, or that which results from a poor self-image, man bears the consequences. There is another place in the Bible where people bore the consequences of their poor self-images. In Numbers 13 we see again the judgment of God because of a poor self image. Moses sent men to spy out the land of Caanan. In verse 33, we read, "There also we saw the Nephilim (the sons of Anak are part of the Nephilim); and we became like grasshoppers in our own sight and so we were in their sight."

They didn't think they were capable of dealing with these giants. They had a poor self-image. They didn't feel strong enough, competent enough, nor did they have enough trust in God to be able to handle the situation. Because of this, they died in the wilderness.

There are other places in Scripture which make reference to a poor self-image, leaving no doubt that this topic is dealt with in God's Word. However, the way in which churches handle this problem is in itself a problem, and this gives cause for Hunt and McMahon to come against the concept. Some churches have "psychologized" the problem, working to help people build a personal self-image. This approach moves into secular humanism, and that is a part of the New Age; thus, it is occult.

God has provided another solution to this problem: we must learn who we are in Christ. What does Jesus say about those who have received Him as Lord and Savior? What has He made us? Our esteem and confidence come from being transformed by the renewal of our minds to agree with what Jesus says about us. If you are feeling rejection, He has received you. If you are feeling inferior, He has made you superior. You are MORE THAN A CONQUERER through Him who lives you. If you are feeling unlovable, He has made you lovable. If you are feeling sinful, He has made you to be the righteousness of God in Christ Jesus.

And so, our self-image has to become God's image of us — what God says about us — not what we say about ourselves. Many teachers have used psychological teaching to help overcome that poor self-image, and in so doing, they have promoted secular humanism. Hunt and McMahon see this and rightfully say, "Wait a minute! We're supposed to be trusting God." But when they then state that there is no such thing as a poor self-image, they are wrong. When they claim that some men are treating this condition by means of human psychology, or humanistic psychology, they are right — they are! The condition needs to be treated with the Word of

God. We need to be "force-fed" with the Word of God until we know who we are in Christ Jesus.

Today, I am not the same person I was when Jesus saved me. I am learning to become what He says I am, and everyday I am being transformed into that image.

We have to conclude that there is error on both sides. We cannot come against the use of psychology in building up the self-image by saying there is no such thing as a poor self-image. It is biblical. A poor self-image causes many Christians to suffer severely and hinders their doing the will of God. When people do not know who they are in Christ, the Body of Christ is crippled, because these people do not believe themselves to be capable, qualified, competent, or able. Therefore, they are not doing anything in power for the Lord Jesus Christ.

THE COMING REVIVAL

Hunt and McMahon indicate that they do not believe in the coming great revival (page 65, "Departure from the Faith or from the Earth?"). "Paul's prophecy of apostasy (the falling away of believers from their original beliefs) seems to fly in the face of the prevailing optimacy and predictions of great revival that dominate Christian media." The authors say that we are not going to have the great revival, that we are not going to take over places of authority in this earth, that we are not going to be in power as Christians. They seem to feel that we are going to be under constant pressure, suffering oppression, with things going from bad to worse until Christ comes to rapture us out of all of it.

Christ is going to rapture us out, but we are also told in Joel's prophecy that God is going to pour out His Spirit on all flesh, and that hasn't happened yet. It didn't appear at the first Pentecost (in the upper room), it didn't happen at the second Pentecost, and it hasn't happened at the third Pentecost. It hasn't happened yet!

There are many other prophecies in the Old Testament which speak of the coming revival that will sweep the face of the earth. That revival hasn't been seen yet. So — both views are right: there will be a great revival, and Jesus will come to rapture us. Jesus himself said, "Occupy until I come," which means do your best — occupy! Don't hover around in some corner, saying, "We're going to suffer until Jesus comes." Occupy! Hunt and McMahon err in saying that the predictions of revival are not scriptural. These predictions are definitely scriptural. There will be a revival that will cover the face of the earth, according to Joel's prophecy.

The authors suggest that Christians are being seduced by the teaching of a coming revival and by "success" teaching. They say that God doesn't want us to be a success — He wants to be spiritual. Yet, this teaching also falls under "occupy until I come." In Joshua 1, God gives us a plan so that we can succeed. Forms of the words "success" and "prosperity" are found throughout Scripture. All of the patriarchs prospered, as did the kings and faithful priests. God promised prosperity to the patriarchs prior to the Law, and in the Law He promised prosperity to the Jews. (See Deuteronomy 6, 7, 8.) And in Galatians 3:14, we are promised the blessings of Abraham. The only problem lies in our interpretation of what success and prosperity are. There is no way, however, to say that success teaching is not biblical!

"WE ARE GODS"

The next major question relates to the teaching that we are gods. If you saw the movie, **The Gods of the New Age,** you very clearly saw this teaching in Eastern religion. On page 84, the authors speak of the fact that there is a new emphasis on this teaching by some faith teachers. They spell the word with a little "g," but they still say we are little gods. Hunt and McMahon refer to two scriptures which say this: John 10:34 and Psalm 82:6. Beside the second verse I have written in the margin, "DPI." Those who have attended our seminary know what these initials mean — DON'T PREACH IT! Certain things in the Word of God are too hot and too clumsy to be handled. We have so little information on them that if we preach in that area, we could get ourselves into a lot of trouble, serving only to confuse people.

Some brothers in the Body of Christ are preaching things that I am afraid to preach, because I simply don't have enough information on them. We certainly don't have enough upon which to build a biblical doctrine. I have seen, historically, that every time people have preached "you are gods," or "you are the manifest sons of God," such massive error has been produced that many people in the Body of Christ have been injured by it. This is truly what has happened, although we may not like to admit this, since the Word says, "the world is waiting for the manifest sons of God." This is a positive statement, yet, every time it is preached, something negative or harmful seems to come out of it.

The ultimate end of the teaching of the "sons of God" has been the extremism of positive confession: "Since I am the manifest son of God, I am a god myself (under God, but still a god, myself), and anything I say must come to pass. If I say, 'Cadillac appear,' soon a Cadillac will drive up and open its door." This is what has come from some of those who profess to be Manifest Sons of God. Then they begin to move into the control of other people. They believe they can confess over others, and what they confess will come to pass. For example, "You give me money." I believe all of this is just as Hunt and McMahon say it is — an occult practice.

As you can well imagine, most who come under the teaching of the Manifest Sons of God do not stay with it very long. It takes about five years before people come to realize how stupid they have been, because ultimately they realize the hard, cold fact that everything that comes out of their mouths does not come to pass. Just speaking the words doesn't make it happen, and they soon find out that they are not the gods they were told they were. In the beginning, people get excited about the concept, and they go off by themselves so they won't hear any negative thinking — or preaching. They refuse to listen to any teaching except from those who preach "manifest sons of God." They get caught up in trying to make things happen, and five years down the road, when they realize nothing is happening, they drop out.

Let's see what God's Word says in Psalm 82:

God takes His stand in His own congregation; He judges in the midst of the rulers.

2 How long will you judge unjustly, And show partiality to the wicked? Selah.

3 Vindicate the weak and fatherless; Do justice to the afflicted and destitute.

4 Rescue the weak and needy; Deliver them out of the hand of the wicked.

5 They do not know nor do they understand; They walk about in darkness; All the foundations of the earth are shaken.

6 I said, "You are gods, And all of you are sons of the Most High.

"Arise, oh God, judge the earth for it is Thou who dost possess all the nations." That is what the Psalmist is saying in the last line. Verse six says, "You are gods," using the word "elohim," which means the Lord God Almighty in every other place. God is saying, "Ye are gods." Hunt and McMahon believe this indicates that we have made ourselves to be gods. Yet, that is not the context. Essentially, it says, "You are gods, but nevertheless, you are going to die like Me."

"You are gods!" God said it. It is the Word! We have to face the fact that it is there — God said it. He said it to the Jews. All of the scholars down through the centuries who have had both feet on the floor have determined that what He meant was, "I have made you gods. By giving you the Word and the truth and the power and light, I have placed My power in your midst and therefore, you have become like Me."

Hunt and McMahon take this back to the Garden of Eden, saying that when Adam and Eve ate of the forbidden fruit, they become as gods. That is what satan promised them. Satan cannot make anyone a god — only God can make you a god. It isn't satan who is saying that you are gods — it is God who says you are!

John 10:31-36 tells us:

31 The Jews took up stones again to stone Him.

32 Jesus answered them, "I showed you many good works from the Father; for which of them are you stoning Me?"

33 The Jews answered Him, "For a good work we do not stone

You, but for blasphemy; and because You, being a man, make Yourself out to be God."

34 Jesus answered them, "Has it not been written in your Law, 'I SAID YOU ARE GODS?'"

35 "If he called them gods, to whom the word of God came (and the Scripture cannot be broken).

36 Do you say of Him, whom the Father sanctified and sent into the world, 'You are blaspheming,' because I said, 'I am the Son of God'?

That tells us exactly why God called them "gods." They were called "gods" because the Word of God was given to them. It had nothing to do with the forbidden fruit, as it argued in **The Seduction of Christianity**. It has to do with the fact that they had the Word of God — so they were gods.

The truth of the matter is that, according to this scripture, believers are gods. The problem with this is that as soon as you begin thinking that, you are in trouble. The end result of such thinking is seen in what the New Age, the Buddhists, and the Hindus are doing — puffing themselves up and glorifying themselves because they have opened themselves to the pride of life. And that is sin.

The thinking goes like this: "If God calls me a god, then I am a god — so watch out for me because here I come!" That is wrong! That is pride! There is great danger in that attitude, and this is why my Bible says DPI — don't preach it!

I can't apologize for God's telling us that we are gods — it is in the Word. I can't tell any of the faith teachers that they shouldn't preach it — because it is scriptural. But I am not going to teach it, because I cannot see how we can benefit from teaching that particular doctrine. We have not yet arrived at being the "manifest sons of God." We may be there some-day, but we haven't reached that point yet.

This whole concept of being gods is difficult. I can see why it is attacked in **The Seduction of Christianity,** because it can result in New Age think-ing. New Age leaders would have us believe that all of us are little gods. They try to have us bow down to all the people who are saying they are gods. That is why all the gurus have so many people following them — they believe these gurus are gods, when there is only ONE GOD ALMIGHTY.

Because this is such a difficult area, you need to use discernment. You should not rebuke those who are teaching it, but be very cautious about what is being taught. Use discernment. Recognize the fact that you may not be able to handle going around confessing that you are a god — even though you are confessing the Word. It could be very dangerous for you.

Others may disagree with me on this matter, but this is where I stand personally. There is a divergence of opinion. You have Hunt and

McMahon's opinion, you have my opinion, and there are still other opinions. But this difference of opinion exists because there is not enough in the Scripture to give us a basis for dealing with this issue with absolute assurance.

POSITIVE CONFESSION

The authors say that if we are to be saved, we must confess that we have sinned by trying to play God (page 88). They claim that positive confession is being preached as a substitute for confession of sin. They say that faith teachers would have us confess our healing, our prosperity, our divine right, and the command God to heal and to bless. They say, further, that such confession if not repentance which qualifies for the forgiveness that God offers by virtue of the fact that Christ paid the full penalty for our rebellion. They say that this is a positive confession which is a renewed declaration that we want the same Godhood that satan offered to Eve.

Apart from a couple of leaders, I do not know of many teachers who do not bring people to confess their sin. I have heard both Kenneth Hagin and Kenneth Copeland lead people to confess their sin in order to receive salvation. I've heard other faith teachers lead people to Christ through the sinner's prayer. These same leaders then had people confess who they are now in Jesus Christ, which is positive biblical confession.

In **The Seduction of Christianity**, the authors come against positive confession in several places. They are especially concerned about confessing healing while a person may still have obvious signs of an illness. They claim that those who do this are practicing shamanism, that they are deceived and into the occult. I have heard Dave Hunt ridicule those who say, "I am healed," when there is still sickness and disease in their bodies. Yet, my Bible says, "By Jesus' stripes I WAS healed."

The Word of God also says that I am saved. There are three tenses involved in the salvation message: I was saved, I am saved, and I will be saved. I am not in heaven yet, nor is Dave Hunt. Yet he confesses that he is saved. Why? Because he was saved, he is saved, and he will be saved. The word for salvation in the Greek includes healing, salvation and deliverance. All these things are included in the same word. You cannot separate one from the other, because the Greek word means all three.

Therefore, saying, "I was healed, I am healed, and I will be healed" is a very proper and positive biblical statement to make. "I was healed nearly 2,000 years ago on the cross. I may have sickness symptoms in my body, but I was healed on the cross. (In like manner, "I was saved nearly 2,000 years ago on the cross. I am still here on earth, but I shall be in heaven because I was saved on the cross.")

The problem encountered in this is due to the counterfeit, which is seen in the teaching of Christian Science practitioners, who say that there is no sickness, there is no disease, there is no death. ("This arm isn't broken — it is a figment of my imagination.") You may have heard the story of the man who meets another fellow and asks, "How is your friend?"

"Oh, he is really sick."

The first man objects: "He just thinks he is sick." He met the same fellow a week later and asked the same question: "How is your friend?"

"Oh, he thinks he is dead!"

This is how I understand Christian Science. It is totally different from a positive biblical confession which states: "By the stripes of Jesus Christ, I am healed. I was healed nearly 2,000 years ago. I am healed by Jesus' stripes, and these symptoms will go out of my body, and I will be healed." That is an absolutely proper biblical confession, and there is no way to come against it. Yet, Hunt frowns on it on the basis that he has seen similar confession in Christian Science. He calls it shamanism, an occult practice. He says we are doing the same thing as is found in Christian Science practice, but it is not the same at all. It is totally different — Christian Scientists deny reality, we say God changes reality.

TRUTH MIXED WITH ERROR

Hunt and McMahon talk about God giving us the power of choice so that we can freely respond to His love. (See page 104). They further state that the Lord will not violate our promise that God makes. They affirm that if you believe God and His promises that say you are going to be saved, then you will be saved, because God is faithful to His promise. They then suggest that you cannot be certain that God will answer any other prayer. Therefore, they negate the rest of the Word, by saying that you can trust one promise but cannot trust any other. If we cannot trust God for **ALL** His promises, we cannot trust Him for **ANY** of His promises. God gives up principles and promises. The Scripture says that every word of God proves true. God has promised some things in an "if then" clause: "If you do this — then I will do that." If we then do what He says and pray and belive (**PRAYER** and **BELIEF** are essential), then He will do as He has promised. If we do our part, God will do His. Either we can trust Him for this, or else, every word of God does not prove true.

Scripture also says that every promise of God is "yea and amen, in Jesus." This means every promise is fulfilled in Jesus Christ — each one is true in Christ Jesus. Galatians says that the blessings of Abraham are ours. Now if that is true, you can trust God for His promises. We must be able to trust **ALL** His promises. God operates by His rules and principles. Why did Jesus have to die on the cross? Couldn't God have found some other way to save us? If we think about it, it seems like such a ridiculous thing to do — He made His Son die on the cross to save us! He could just have said, "Be saved." He did not **HAVE** to have Jesus die on the cross — but

He **DID** have to. There was a reason for that supreme sacrifice: there was a rule. The rule said that there was no forgiveness without the shedding of blood. God made Himself subject to His own rules. He chose that — we didn't. We didn't say He had to do it that way — He chose to do it that way. We would have looked for another way. But God did not — He chose to follow His own rule.

In the Psalms, we read that God has highly exalted His Word. One version reads "above His name." Another reads, "along with His name." The truth of the matter is that in the Hebrew, His word is equivalent to His name. He has highly exalted His Word and His name. What He has spoken is firm — it will not pass away. We can trust it, we can believe it. If we cannot, then we are all in trouble.

If we cannot trust His Word, then all we would be left with is man's opinion. It would be every man for himself. We would not be able to expect anything from God. Then we would have to go as a worm to God and beg and plead with tears and fasting, whenever we wanted to ask Him for anything. There would be no other way, unless He just happened to feel good at that moment and decide He wanted to grant our requests.

God has set some principles in motion. He has spoken His Word. He has said, "This is the way it is," and He will abide by His Word, because He spoke it, and His Word is as good as His name. This is His choice — we didn't make these rules — He did!

VISUALIZATION

The next major area of concern is visualization. (See page 140 in the book.) There is a problem here, because one of the key experiences in the occult and the New Age is visualization. People caught up into the occult visualize things, believing that they can think them into existence. The authors say that visualization cannot be used in Christian circles because there is no example of it in the Bible: therefore, it is an occult practice. Remember, an argument from silence is not a good argument, so you must look further.

It is important to clarify what we mean by visualization. The problem may well lie in semantics. Mark 11:23 says that if you believe in your heart and do not doubt, it will come to pass. The next verse says that if you believe that you have received you shall receive. What does this mean? If you can't see the end result of that thing in reality in your imagination, if you can't visualize that thing being done, you won't believe that you will receive it. There is no other way you can believe that you receive without imagining it — without seeing it in your mind's eye, without visualizing it. If you do not see it as done, nothing will happen, according to Mark 11. Visualizing is not occult!

The other problem we encounter in this area is that there is no biblical example of what any saint was doing in his mind when he prayed. The Bible simply does not address that subject. We do not know how Jesus thought as He prayed. We do not know what was going on inside of His Spirit and mind. We do not know what was going on inside Paul's mind when he was reading, and thinking, and speaking, and praying. We just do not know these things. Every person of faith in the Bible could have visualized a thing as done, and we would have no way of knowing it. Thus, we cannot say, "It isn't in the Scripture, therefore, it isn't right."

Since Mark 11 says, "Believe that it is done and that you have received it," we have to consider how we are going to do that. Somehow we have to visualize the thing as done. That is very different from occult visualization, because occult visualization says, "Because I visualize it, it is done!"

Scripture says, that because you visualize, it and believe in God, and have faith in God, and trust God — God will surely bring it to pass. The difference is great. One approach makes me God, the other approach makes Him God, and I am simply getting into agreement with Him. Both of these approaches sound alike; they both look very, very similar. So, if we come against all Christians who are saying that visualization is a good technique to activate our prayer life, we then put them under unjust condemnation. The book refers to such people as shamans, witches, and wizards. We cannot do that. Every human being uses visualization when he speaks. When I say "horse," what do you see? A stallion? A palamino? A pony? How about when I say "dog?" Do you see a hairy, yippie, little lap dog? Or a viscious Doberman? We all visualize constantly. We cannot draw a picture without first visualizing it. Therefore, why should it be wrong for us to visualize when we pray? The only problem arises when we believe that we can create by our visualization alone, apart from God.

THE WORDS WE SPEAK AND THE THOUGHTS WE THINK

Hunt and McMahon state that many Christians believe that the words and thoughts become vehicles of spiritual power. (See page 149.) They feel that those who accept that concept are victims of a great delusion which, again, replaces God with ourselves. In Proverbs 13:2 we read "From the fruit of a man's mouth, he enjoys good." Proverbs 12:14 essentially states the same premise: "A man will be satisfied with good by the fruit of his words. And the deeds of a man's hands will return to Him." There are other scriptures, too, which tell us that the words which we speak have power. Our words have the "power of life and death."

The words that we speak do become vehicles of spiritual power — for good, or for evil. In a very practical sense, when we speak words to our children which tell them, "You're stupid, you're ugly, you are never going to amount to anything," we are damaging their souls. When they grow up, they are going to perceive themselves to be stupid, ugly and worthless. Our words have power and can speak death to them.

The fact that I believe this does not mean that I am under some delusion, and I am not replacing God with myself. I am acknowledging a reality that we can see with our eyes in the world, and read for ourselves in the Word of God. Yes! Words do have power!

Those in the occult say that our words have much more power than this. Some of the Manifest Sons of God say that our words have much more power than this. There are, however, limitations to what we can do with our words. We simply cannot create a new world. We cannot say, "Let planet Xaton come into being," and have it appear. We cannot say, "Let there be an apple," and have an apple come into our hand. That is occult. That is New Age. That is heresy! But to say, "I'm going to eat well, and I am going to speak good, so that things are going to improve in my life, and I am going to produce better," — that is no occult. That is Bible! That is practical Bible application. That works for occult people, that works for Christian people. The rain falls on the just and the unjust. It happens!

Words have the power to shape attitudes. When people speak negatively to their children, they grow up with negative attitudes. When they speak positively to their offspring, they grow up with a positive attitude and a feeling of self-worth.

Our thoughts, as well as our words, have power. If you doubt this, try being a salesman sometimes, or try sharing the Word of God, by starting with the attitude, "They are not going to listen to me. They are not going to accept what I say. Why should I even talk to them?" If you begin on that basis, you will talk yourself out of it even before you go! When you get the appointment, you don't want to approach them by saying, "I don't suppose you want to receive Jesus." If you think you can't, then you can't. That is why the Word says, "Be transformed by the renewing of your mind."

Our words are going to produce the atmosphere. Our words are going to produce success, or lack of success, in us. They DO have impact! That is not an illusion. That is not replacing God with self. That is simply acknowledging a biblical truth. But we have to realize that there is a limit to what we can accomplish with our words. God wants us to speak and think positively about ourselves and about other people. Agree with God and His promises. But, if we believe we can create by our words alone, we have stepped over into the occult. Don't put down positive confession for the sake of staying away from the occult.

Hunt and McMahon (on page 149) declare that we are ignoring biblical warnings against occultism, and we are willing to accept psychological theories, success formulas, and shamanistic visualization that are neither scientific or biblical, because we do not recognize their occult nature. What he is actually saying is that there are no success formulas in the Bible.

Joshua 1:5-9 says:

5 No man will be able to stand before you all the days of your life. Just as I have been with Moses, I will be with you; I will not fail you or forsake you.

6 Be strong and courageous, for you shall give this people possession of the land which I swore to their fathers to give them.

7 "Only be strong and very courageous; be careful to do according to all the law which Moses My servant commanded you; do not turn from it to the right or to the left, so that you may have success wherever you go.

8 This book of the law shall not depart from your mouth, but you shall meditate on it day and night, so that you may be careful to do according to all that is written in it; for then you will make your way prosperous, and then you will have success.

9 "Have I not commanded you? Be strong and courageous! Do not tremble or be dismayed, for the Lord your God is with you wherever you go."

Now that is a success formula. It ends by saying, essentially, "If you do what I have told you to do here, you will make your way prosperous." That is not occult. That is the Word of God! That is a formula for success.

There are times when God says, "I will prosper your way if you do what I tell you to do." There are times when He says, "YOU prosper your way if you do what I tell you to do." Either way, it is a success formula. "Do this and you are going to have prosperity." There are many God-given success formulas!

POSITIVE AND POSSIBILITY THINKING

We have already touched on this theme, but I would like to add the following. Matthew 21:21, 22 says, "If you have faith, and do not doubt, . . .you shall receive." If you do not believe that it is possible, you are a doubter. This is impossibility thinking! But if you believe it is possible, if you have faith and do not doubt, you have possibility thinking. Things will only come to pass when you are in agreement with God. You must know what He says and believe that it is possible. "God said it in His Word, I believe it in my heart and I believe it is possible." If you don't have possibility thinking, you are not going to trust God to do anything. You will only go as far as your self-image will let you go, but you won't trust God for anything.

SELF-TALK

On page 154, Hunt and McMahon concede that our thoughts influence us in many ways, but that thinking, speaking, and visualizing do not have virtually unlimited power. They further state that there are no biblical methods which use thinking, speaking, and visualization to release God's power. Yes, they are right, and no, they are not right. Thinking, speaking, and visualization do not have the unlimited power that has been attributed to them by some. That is absolutely true — some people have gone beyond reason. They have gone beyond the Word of God. They have gotten close to, if not into, the occult and the New Age teaching. However, there are biblical methods for releasing God's power, using thinking, speaking, and visualizing.

Following this, Hunt and McMahon discuss the concept of self-talk. Let me tell you about self-talk. Matthew 5:28 gives us the story of the woman with the flow of blood. The Greek says that this woman continually said, "If I can just touch the hem of Jesus' garment, I will be healed." The Greek is very clear. It cannot be denied. This woman continually built up her belief by speaking the words of faith. This is self-talk. She spoke faith and built her faith by speaking. She confessed that if she could just touch the hem of his garment, she would be saved.

In the account of Job's life, we see the truth of the thing he feared the most coming upon him. Job was exercising a negative faith. It has been proven scientifically that a good attitude makes a great deal of difference in health and other areas of our personal life. Most hospitals administer an attitude scan to decide whether a person is a good candidate for a heart transplant. It has been found that people with a poor attitude are high-risk candidates, while people with a positive attitude have a good chance of recovering fully from a heart transplant.

A good attitude, self-talk, believing and speaking positive things according to the Word, can change the course of your life. What does it mean to "meditate on the Word?" Keep the Word before you. The Bible says to meditate upon it day and night.

In Joshua we read, "Do not let it depart from your mouth." That is self-talk; that is talking to yourself to renew your mind. We must speak the Word, and speak it into ourselves. We must not let it depart from our mouths. We must keep speaking it day and night. That form of self-talk is a biblical principle.

To whom was David speaking, when he said, "Why are you disquieted, oh, my soul?" and "Praise the Lord, oh, my soul"?

Who was he talking to? He was talking to himself. He was saying, "Get out of this grumpy mood that you're in. Get out of the morbid thinking. Get with it. Get with the program. Praise God, oh, my soul." That is exactly what he was doing, so self-talk is definitely a biblical principle.

VISUALIZING JESUS

The authors express concern about visualizing Jesus (page 162). One of the difficulties here is that we do not know exactly what they are talking about. We don't know exactly what the Bible is talking about. In Hebrews 2:9 we read, "We see Jesus now." See Him? We certainly don't see Him physically now. We see Him in our mind's eye, and we visualize Him —

that is how we see Him. That is what it means.

The authors warn us that if we call on a visualization of Jesus and seek such a visualization, we will get a demon. My Bible, in Luke 11:10-13, says something that I can trust:

> 10 "For everyone who asks, receives; and he who seeks, finds; and to him who knocks, it shall be opened.
>
> 11 "Now suppose one of you fathers is asked by his son for a fish; he will not give him a snake instead of a fish, will he?
>
> 12 "Or if he is asked for an egg, he will not give him a scorpion, will he?
>
> 13 "If you then, being evil, know how to give good gifts to your children, how much more shall your heavenly Father give the Holy Spirit to those who ask him?"

If you ask for the Holy Spirit, are you afraid you are going to get a demon? No, God says you don't have to worry about it. If you ask for Jesus, are you afraid you are going to get an evil spirit? No, because you are calling upon the name of the Lord. Otherwise, I would be afraid to ever call upon the Lord in prayer, because a demon might respond to me. I would be afraid to pray for anybody to receive the baptism of the Holy Spirit, because he might receive an evil spirit. This is one of the arguments that satan gives to people: "Don't ask for the Holy Spirit — you are liable to receive a demon." If you have ever prayed for people to receive the baptism of the Holy Spirit, you have probably heard that argument. That is not the way God works; if you ask for the Holy Spirit, you get the Holy Spirit. If you ask for Jesus, you don't get a demon!

HEALING OF MEMORIES

If you have had any background in the healing of the memories, you realize there is some strange stuff going on in this area. Visualization is used a lot. The participant is told to visualize Jesus being there, back in a situation in his life when he was really hurting, when he was molested or beaten or robbed, or when his parents did something to him. He is told to visualize Jesus laying hands on him and ministering to him, or Jesus expressing His love to him, or Jesus expressing forgiveness for that situation.

Now this could be considered strange, and if you look at it from the occult perspective of visualization, you would be thinking about changing past history by some vision. The one who is involved in healing of the memories is, in his understanding, trying to make Jesus real at a time when he was hurting. The one who needs healing could not seem to experience Jesus in the situation at that former time, so he is trying to go back and experience Jesus' healing touch at that time and make it real to himself in the present. And — it works! People who hurt can receive forgiveness and healing.

When the authors are talking about the healing of the memories, they have reason to be skeptical of what is going on because some of it borders on occult practice and most of what some leaders have taught about it was absolute rubbish from the New Age — literally, Eastern religion. However, what most Christians have done is to take what appears to be positive and acceptable to Christians and use it to help many people. I have never known anyone who has been put in bondage by the healing of the memories. I am not justifying everything that goes on under the name of healing of memories, but I am saying there are some good people who practice the healing of memories without going to the extremes — extremes which could be considered occult.

To say that Jesus is not concerned about our memories is neither accurate nor biblical. He judged Saul for his memories of events from his past. Saul had an alternative. Saul had to be able to trust God to heal those memories and past pains, or he could never have gotten judged for them. So God does care about our past memories, but we have to use discernment to determine what is acceptable and what is not.

I heard a story of the healing of the memories by one of the great men in a recent revival in England. It was about a fellow who could not receive forgiveness. he could not accept forgiveness for past mistakes, so this pastor drew a cross on the wooden floor with chalk and said, "Does the Bible say that your sins were nailed to the cross when Jesus was nailed to the cross?" (The Bible does say our sins were nailed to the cross.) The pastor said, "Okay, take a hammer and nails and pound the nails into that cross and name your sin."

The man began to pound nails into the cross on that floor and name his sin. He broke and received the forgiveness of the Lord. That actual act made the whole thing real to him. He was visualizing in actuality something that helped him to receive the reality of Jesus' grace. All we need to do is say it, believe it and receive it. You wouldn't call that "occult" practice just because this pastor did something out of the ordinary. Surely that method was wisdom from God, to help the man see that "Yes, indeed, my sin was **NAILED** to the cross, and it is over and done."

EXTREMES

Hunt and McMahon (see page 174) make reference in their book to a precious brother in the Lord, John Wimber, preceded by the following quote from his lecture notes for a course entitled "Signs and Wonders:"

At the time of the preparation of this manual, Dr. C. Peter Wagner and I have been teaching MC 510 for three years. It has been one of the most invigorating and exciting adventures of our lives.

At his date, January 1985, we have had in excess of 700 students take the course at Fuller Seminary School of World Missions. The

results have been astounding. Better than 90 percent of the students
have indicated a paradigm shift in which they are now ministering in
an altered worldview.

Because John Wimber uses the words, "worldview," and "paradigm
shift," he is labeled an occultist. What does he mean by these words? MC
510 is a course concerned with winning the world for Jesus Christ
(through the power of the Holy Spirit and the gifts of the Spirit) in an
evangelical seminary, where the gifts have never been recognized. Wimber
went into that place and began to teach that we cannot be Christians confined to the four walls of our church buildings, but we have to be world
Christians, concerned about the world, and we have to take the power of
the Living God to the world.

Most of the students at Fuller are evangelical, but those who have taken
MC 510 have learned about the gifts and the ministry of the Holy Spirit.
They have had a paradigm shift — a shift in understanding, a shift in
thought pattern — so that they have stopped thinking about the church
being confined to four walls, and they have started thinking about the
world and world Christianity, and about winning the world for Jesus
Christ by getting out there and saving people through the power of the
Holy Spirit.

Signs and Wonders is one of the most powerful courses that has ever
been taught in any seminary. It is straight down the line, right on, but
because John Wimber uses the words "worldview" and "paradigm shift,"
he is considered by some to be an occultist!

The authors further speak of the fact that John Wimber practices inner
healing in his own church. I practice inner healing — no occult practice,
no hypnotism — but healing of the memories and the resultant hurts by
asking Jesus to take away the hurt and heal the memories.

John Wimber is a precious brother in the Lord. He is not a faith teacher,
not an occultist, not a weirdo. He has recommended books that some
may question, but that does not remove him from the rank of brother,
nor does it make him an occultist.

THE SUBCONSCIOUS

The authors would have us believe that there is no such thing as the
subconscious. That is a lie perpetrated by humanistic psychology. The
Scripture talks to us about the mind of the flesh, the mind of the soul, and
the mind of the body. David says he speaks to his soul, and his spirit
speaks to his soul. In Romans 7, we see a battle going on between the
mind of the flesh and the mind of the spirit. We discover there is a mind of
the heart. Jesus talks to us about the mind of the heart, and the mind, in
general.

Because the actual word, "subconscious" is not used in Scripture, the authors deny its existence. Where do our dreams come from, if they are not from God or satan? From the conscious mind? Our conscious mind is asleep — so where could they be coming from? The subconscious is an obvious reality, and is included in the several different mind within our being which Jesus teaches us about. It is difficult to understand why anyone would say there is no such thing as the subconscious mind.

HUMANISTIC PSYCHOLOGY

When Hunt and McMahon come against humanistic psychology, I am the first to shout, "Hallelujah! Amen!" Humanistic psychology is occult — it is detrimental to the Church — and there is no place for it in the Body of Christ. I was a psychology major in college, graduating with a degree in that subject. In my first church, I sent a letter to the members of my congregation, saying, "I am qualified and competent to handle problems in all these areas." I added, "I am available to you by phone and for walk-ins." I gave them specific times when I would be available. Nobody came! Not one soul! Nobody called!

I prayed, "I thought I should be the best psychologist possible to be a good pastor. How come nobody is coming? I am doing my best." I sensed the Lord answered with a question: "Who called you to be a psychologist? I called you to be a pastor and preach **MY** Word, not humanistic psychology." At that point, I did not know there was anything wrong with it. No one had ever told me. I wasn't in the Full Gospel teaching at the time. Then God told me.

Because of this, I went back and checked out what I had learned in college and compared it to the Word of God and found that 98 percent of it was absolute trash. It was humanisitc garbage that had no place at all in the Body of Christ. Healing comes through the Word of God; healing comes through forgiveness, and the blood of the Lamb; healing comes through the cross, and I will stand next to Dave Hunt and shout, "Amen!" when he preaches that.

Each of us has a subconscious mind, and we need to recognize that. There is an inferiority complex and it needs to be dealt with biblically, not humanistically. Some of the brothers who have learned special techniques in counseling through their psychology courses are great brothers who have sorted through the biblical principles. They know the difference between humanistic secular psychology and biblical psychology. These men understand there is a counterfeit.

The authors refer (on page 187) to the fact that numerous Christians suffer in varying degrees from frustration, worry, habits, regrets, guilt, resentment, insecurity, and a whole range of negative feelings. We must be able to minister to these needs with well-trained biblical counselors. Let us not condemn the Christian psychologists who know the truth and are trying hard to help those in need.

IN CONCLUSION

I have wept and travailed before God as to what is truth and what is error. The things I have said here are not to put another man down. David
Hunt and T.A. McMahon have done the Church a service in bringing
aspects of Christianity before the Body of Christ so that we have been
forced to go back and discern what is right and wrong for each of us
before God.

My words come from my thoughts. My concern is that you do not accept my words or Hunt's and McMahon's words without prayerfully
discerning the truth through the Word of God.

I have only scratched the surface of the issues raised because of limited
time. You will have to discern the rest for yourself. Do not condemn
anyone on the basis of what you read in **The Seduction of Christianity.**
Judge each ministry by its fruit, according to the Word of God. May the
Spirit lead you into all truth!

CRITIQUE OF
THE SEDUCTION OF CHRISTIANITY

By Mark Virkler

Along with his responsibilities as Dean of Students, Director of Curriculum Development, teacher and author of more than 25 books, Mark Virkler has a traveling schedule which involves doing Communion With God Seminars, every other weekend somewhere in the U.S., Canada or Great Britain. In these seminars he trains Christians how to clearly hear the voice of God, as well as how to clearly see the vision of God, birthed within their hearts by the Holy Spirit. (See International Leaders comments at end of book).

My heart was deeply grieved as I encountered the accusations flowing through the book which I was reading. The book, recently published by Harvest House, attacked many of the most significant spiritual leaders in the Church today. Paul Yonggi Cho, Robert Schuller, Dr. Kenneth Hagin, Earl Paulk, Robert Tilton, Charles Capps, Frederick Price, Kenneth Copeland, Norman Grubb, Bill Volkman, Agnes Sanford, Ralph Wilkerson, John and Paula Sanford, Richard Foster, Morton Kelsey, C.S. Lovett, Rita Bennett, Dennis and Matt Linn, Ruth Carter Stapleton, John Wimber, Francis MacNutt, James Dobson and others.

What man could possibly have the audacity to touch such a vast array of God's anointed and call them down one after the other, describing how each one has been "seduced" by the cult philosophies of our time? What do all of these people have in common that would throw them into one group for criticism and censure?

The man is author Dave Hunt, and the book is his current release, **The Seduction of Christianity.** The thing held in common by these men is that they believe in having a positive mental attitude. They also believe that they can see in the spirit the visions of almighty God and speak them forth in a creative way. Thirdly, they believe that Christians become expressions of God to the world in which they live, and fourthly, these men have a worldview that believes that light is advancing rather than darkness. These beliefs do not strike me as being cultish. As a matter of fact, I have found nearly a thousand verses that substantiate these beliefs.

Dave Hunt reasons that since some cults hold the above-mentioned beliefs, any Chrstian who also believes these things must have been seduced by the teachings of these cults. It strikes me as totally backward to **first** discern what cults believe and **then** hold up church leaders to these beliefs to see if they have been influenced by them. A much more sound practice would be to examine what the Bible teaches on these subjects and then hold up the beliefs of these men to the teaching of Scripture.

Since the book has such great power to confuse and persuade, I am offering the following critique of it.

STRENGTHS

1. David Hunt is obviously **a scholar concerning the beliefs of modern day cults.** He has done much research and is to be commended for his research ability.

2. This book will cause all Christians to be **more aware of the possibility of deception** in the age in which we live, and therefore will inspire all Christians to take a deeper look at the biblical foundation for their beliefs.
3. This book will **help Christians clarify and deepen the messages** in the areas in which he attacks. Thus the end product will have value.

WEAKNESSES

1. Because Dave Hunt has spent so much time studying cults, he **focuses first on the beliefs of cults (rather than Scripture).** He compares the teaching of outstanding Christian leaders, such as Paul Yonggi Cho, Robert Schuller, Kenneth Hagin and Earl Paulk against what cults believe, rather than against what the Bible teaches. This is a **backward approach** for testing for error and a fundamental flaw in his book.

2. **Mr. Hunt is not a "Berean,"** in that a Berean "examines the Scriptures daily, to see whether these things are **SO.**" Whenever Dave Hunt does go to Scripture, he seeks to prove that these things are **NOT SO,** rather than examining the truth in them. For example, when coming against the belief in a positive mental attitude, David Hunt never once examines Philippians 4:8 or any of the hundreds of verses that speak of the scriptural command to have a positive mental attitude. This then becomes **another fundamental flaw of his book,** in that he is seeking to prove error rather than seeking to prove truth, as did the Bereans.

3. Thirdly, Dave Hunt accuses leader after leader in the Church of today, and **appears more as "the accuser of the brethren" than the comforter.** Accusation is the center of satan's work (Rev. 10:10-12), and the Church needs to be careful not to become his mouthpiece. We have been entrusted with the ministry of reconciliation, not the ministry of destruction.

4. If one would read many of the authors that Dave Hunt quotes, he would find that over and over Dave slants and alters the intent of what the author was saying by about 15 percent. In that way the material is in a sense taken directly from various authors; however unless you have read

these men extensively and with a depth of understanding you will not recognize the 15 percent slant which makes their teachings appear evil when in actuality they are not. Therefore I would suggest that no one take the statements of face value, but instead carefully read a fair amount of material by the church leader being slighted so he can form his own unbiased opinion.

5. Dave Hunt fails to see that **the presence of a counterfeit proves that there is also a real thing, and that this real thing has value.** The book needs a much stronger thrust in describing the real things which are the **alternative** to counterfeit. Let us not just concentrate on what we are against. Instead, let us emphasize what we are for.

WILL YOU STONE THE PROPHETS?

Stephen told the religious people of his day that they had always stoned the prophets God sent to them. And to prove his point, they stoned him on the spot. The religious people of Jesus' day were bound by their way of interpreting Scripture, and so when Jesus tried to open their minds and hearts to a new perspective on the Kingdom and the Messiah, they adamantly refused, even for a moment, to set aside their proof texts and honestly examine the new light Jesus was shedding on certain Old Testament passages. In an effort to maintain religious orthodoxy, they crucified the Son of God on the spot.

OR WILL YOU BE A BEREAN?

We do not have to be bound by our teachings and proof texts. Our reasoning is limited. Our perspectives are often tainted. I have found (later in life) that on many occasions I was wrong on a variety of theological positions, even though I could proof text each position to my satisfaction. Surely everyone reading this can say the same thing about his life.

Therefore, we learn that proof texting a point with Scripture doesn't necessarily prove a thing. Calvinists and Arminianists have been doing it for years and have succeeded in maintaining a divided and broken Body of Christ for several hundred years, both sides being able to prove biblically to their satisfaction that they are right. What do you think is more important to God? Proof texting our current position and maintaining a broken Body, or opening our hearts and minds to new perspectives, seeking with all our hearts to understand them and to discover any and all biblical support and clarification for them?

THE CHOICE IS YOURS

Will you be a Berean and examine Scripture daily to see if there is any truth in these prophetic messages (visualization, union consciousness, positive mental attitude, and The Kingdom Now)? Or will you be as the religious people of Jesus' day, saying "I've never been taught that way," and then go out to stone the message and those who bear it? God help us to stop stoning every prophet He sends us! God help us to become Bereans! I invite you to become a Berean!

AUTHORS TWIST
DEFINITION OF SORCERY*

By Richard W. Dortch

One major problem in **The Seduction of Christianity** is the authors' definition of the key word, "sorcery." In any discussion or debate, there must be a clear agreement on the basic definition of key words.

Their definition, given on page 12 of the book, describes "sorcery" in these words: "In the following pages, when we use that word our intended meaning wil be: any attempt to manipulate reality (internal, external, past, present or future) by various mind-over-matter techniques that run the gamut from alchemy and astrology to positive/possibility thinking."

Using that definition, the authors imply that well-known Christian leaders are practicing sorcery: "Many modern practitioners, including leading Christians, seem unaware of the true nature of the dangerous mind-game they are playing. Sorcery called by any other name is still sorcery" (page 14).

There are, of course, much more precise definitions of the word "sorcery." In the Old Testament, the Hebrew words, *kesheph*: "magic: sorcery, witchcraft" and *kashaph*: "to whisper a spell, i.e., to incant or practice magic: — sorcery, use witchcraft" referred to such men as Jannes and Jambres (Ex. 7-9; 2 Tim. 3:8). Another Hebrew word describing them is *chartom*: "a horoscopist (as drawing magical lines or circles): — magician."

New Testament sorcerers, magicians and those who practiced in occult rites, such as Simon (Acts 8) and Elymas the sorcerer (Acts 13), were linked to the *conscious* practices of divination and magic. The Greek words describing the occult practices are *mageia*: " 'magic': — sorcery" and *mageuo*: "to practice magic: — use sorcery."

Revelation 21:8 and 22:15 say that sorcerers will be excluded from heaven. The Greek word is *pharmakoi*. W.E. Vine says this word, "an adjective signifying 'devoted to magical arts,' is used as a noun, a sorcerer, especially one who uses drugs, potions, spells, enchantments."

Sorcery, according to other Bible passages such as Malachi 3:5 and Revelation 9:21, relate to the practice of dealing *deliberately* with evil spirits.

Likewise, Webster's dictionary definition of the word "sorcery" is very clearcut: "the use of supernatural power over others through the assistance of evil spirits and witchcraft."

When Hunt and McMahon link all positive/possibility thinking, inner healing, visualization and psychology to "sorcery," the authors make an unsound generalization! Webster's "assistance of evil spirits" and the Bible's dealing deliberately with evil spirits are vastly different from their "any attempt to manipulate reality."

Cho, Schuller, Capps, Tilton and other ministries of the gospel who were mentioned in the book—whether one agrees doctrinally with them or not — have not deliverately sought the assistance of evil spirits. They publicly ascribe their teaching on faith and positive thinking to the Lord Jesus Christ.

The next, and possibly most important point, centers on the question, "Who originates everything?"

A basic problem with the philosophy behind the book is the faulty logic tha tallows Satan, by default, to be the originator of such concepts as inner healing, prosperity teaching and visualization.

Let's make this point very clear: God is the Creator and Originator. Satan is the perverter. Just because Satan worshippers pray does not mean that Christians should stop praying.

We need to be very careful not to espouse such things as transcendental meditation. But just because the Hindus promote that type of meditation does not negate the fact that God endorses meditation at least 20 times in the Old and New Testaments, including Genesis 24:63, Joshua 1:8, Psalm 48:9 and Philippians 4:8.

We cannot be naive. There are numerous counterfeits. I join with the authors in being very concerned about Napoleon Hill's "counselors" (page 32) and "Masters" (page 18).

But do we "throw out the baby with the bathwater"? Do we refuse all self-help techniques? Do we stop listening to everything that smacks of positive thinking?

Worship of God is good and proper. Mankind's perverted rituals do not destroy the original for those who desire fellowship with God.

Yes, we must be very careful to avoid "secularizing" Christianity. Too often as the authors imply, some spurious teachers have perverted the truth by attempting to ascribe Christian terms to some sort of false teaching.

At the same time, we cannot cast aside truths just because someone inside the church did not first invent a particular concept.

Whether the automobile inventors and manufacturers admit this truth or not, the knowledge to make cars, I believe, came from God, and I intend to use my car for God's glory. Another person may use his car to promote ungodliness or even witchcraft, but I feel not need to give up my transportation because someone else misuses his.

Who is the originator of all truth? Who gave us medicine, healing, knowledge and energy? Who gave us the greatest Guidebook for all subjects of science, behavior modification and self-improvement? Who sent the Holy Spirit to guide us into all truth? God!

And just because the Bible does not specifically mention computers, psychological techniques, automatic transmissions and telecasts by name does not mean that I must not use them.

Richard W. Dortch is executive director of the PTL Ministries. A veteran missionary and pastor for over three decades, he distinguished himself as superintendent of the Illinois District of the Assemblies of God.

*Reprinted by permission from **Ministries Magazine,** © by Strang Communications Company, Altamont Springs, FL.

AUTHORS BLAST
CHURCH PSYCHOLOGISTS *

By Robert S. Sterling-Smith

An appropriate reply to the accusations aimed at Christian psychologists in **The Seduction of Christianity** should come from a Christian professional who has been trained and certified as a theologian and a clinical psychologist. It is from this dual perspective that many of the book's claims can be evaluted for their validity and reliability. I refer specifically to chapters 10 through 13: "Mental Alchemy"; "Christianized Idolatry?", "Psychological Salvation"; and "Self-Idolatry."

I am among a growing number of committed Christian psychololgists who are making headway in the discipline of a practical integration of their faith and professional practice.

Scripture clearly teaches that we are a community of saints who need each other as members of the family to work our way through life's trouble spots (Rom. 15:1,2; Gal. 6:1,2; Col. 3:12-15; James 5:14-16).

A good Christian psychologist has been prepared to facilitate and apply these scriptural concepts in just the same way that the preacher has been trained to pastor and preach. It is presumptuous and unfair to suggest that Christian psychologists have been corrputed by others in the field who embrace non-Christian concepts. And it is harsh and unrealistic to suggest that no believers need the benefits one trained in mental health can offer.

But the authors say, "All that we need for dealing with such problems is found in the fact that Christ died for our sins and has risen from the dead to live His life in us. No one who has truly received God's love and forgiveness as a sinful rebel can possibly withhold that same love and forgiveness from those who have wronged him. We love and forgive others because of God's love and forgiveness in us. It is that simple" (page 180).

But that fact is that it is not only possible, but all too often true that many Christians do have more unhealthy, unforgiving and unloving relationships going on than they would care to admit. And this is but one area where the Christian psychologist can help the beleaguered believer to appropriate the promises of the gospel and break through the barriers that keep him from experiencing right relationships with others.

It is wonderful to be able to have a sincere, but untrained brother or sister in Christ with whom we can share our trouble spots. But how much better to have a Christian who is trained in the skills which when coupled with the power of the gospel can help us be set free.

The authors' punch line — "The past is taken care of on the basis of our faith in God and the finished work of Christ on the cross" — is true in the courts of heavenly justice. However, in the process of sanctification we walk with Paul in Romans 7.

For a number of years Dave Hunt has been considered as a knowledgeable person in area of cultic activity. However, he is in no way an expert in the fields of psychology and psychological practice. As a certified psychologist it was instantly apparent to me that the authors of this book were in way over their heads.

The evident intent of this book was to alert the church to the presence of tares among the wheat. And no alert Christians, especially Christian psychologists, can deny that Satan's counterfeiting has come uncomfortably close to the truth. There is increasing spiritual warfare around and within the wheat fields of truth. However, believers engaged in this battle must be able to tell the wheat from the tares. It is not good stewardship to uproot the wheat with the tares.

The reader who is aware of what is going on in the disciplines of mental health services would wonder why none of the leading lights in the "integration" movement are ever seriously mentioned. The names of Crabb, Narramore, Collins and Wright do not appear in this book. The growing Christian Association for Psychological Studies and the highly professional **Journal of Psychology and Theology** are mentioned only in passing.

Instead the authors say that Christian psychology "creates an unequal yoke that brings into the church the seductive influence of secular psychology" (pages 30, 31).

A little investigation into the efforts of the men and women, many of whom were trained in Christian colleges and seminaries, who are now working as Christian psychologists, might have tempered such a harsh and judgmental statement.

Robert S. Sterling-Smith, M. Div., Ph.D., is clinical psychologist and director of Christian Counseling Center at Calvary Baptist Church, New York, New York.

*Reprinted by permission from **Ministries Magazine,** © by Strang Communications Company, Altamonte Springs, FL.

IN DEFENSE OF
INNER HEALING*

By William L. de Arteaga

The Seduction of Christianity is a case study in Christian Phariseeism. That is, it is a form of religious thinking and reasoning, similar to that of the biblical Pharisees, which seeks security only in accepted theological ideas and practices.

Phariseeism seeks to evaluate all spiritual experiences by the standard of conventional theology. Jesus, and later Paul, taught their disciples to evaluate spiritual experiences and persons by their fruit (Matt. 7:15-18; Phil 1:9-10). Because they lack an understanding of "fruit testing," the Christian Pharisees assult their opponents with indiscriminate accusations of heresy and ulimately obstruct the work of the Holy Spirit. All of this is done in the name of orthodoxy.

Hunt's attack on those involved in the development of the inner healing ministry (which he cannot understand because of his ignorance of "fruit testing") is one of the most grievous examples of Christian Phariseeism in modern times.

For example, by use of "cut and paste," Hunt changes the fundamental meaning of a case reported by Ruth Carter Stapleton in her book **The Experience of Inner Healing.** Mrs. Stapleton had prayed with and affirmed a young woman who had been an illegitimate and unwanted child. She showed the woman that in spite of the sin of her parents, under God's providence, her *birth* was holy. Hunt claims that Mrs. Stapleton tried to make the *sin* of fornication holy. (Compare the case as reported in **Seduction,** Page 183, and its original citation in **Experience,** pages 22-23). Unfortunately Hunt's entire book is filled with distortions similar to this.

Perhaps the most sustained, distorted and vicious attacks in the whole book are those directed against Mrs. Agnes Sanford, the woman who developed inner healing. Hunt claims that she was a pantheist and a shaman and was responsible for introducing shamanistic practices into Christianity. His accusation of pantheism is based on the assumption that anyone who sees God in nature is a pantheist. The correct definition of a pantheist is one who believes that God is *only* in nature and not a transcendent being. Mrs. Sanford was biblically correct in her belief that God is both in nature and transcends it (Eph. 4:4-6; compare with her position in **The Healing Light,** page 19).

The accusation of shaman is directed at Mrs. Sanford principally because she used and taught the prayer of visualization. Her faulty reasoning is as follows:

. Visualization was not found in the Bible.

. Visualization was not found in Christian literature before it was introduced by Agnes Sanford.

. Visualization can be found in occult literature as a technique of magic.

. Therefore, visualization is occult.

Christians tend to forget that similar arguments were made 200 years ago when Sunday schools were invented. One could repeat Hunt's argument by saying: Sunday schools are not found in the Bible. But schools of occult knowledge have existed in pagan religions (as in the temple schools of Egypt) since the earliest times. Therefore Sunday schools are occult.

In fact, prayer-visualization is of ancient usage in Christian life. St. Bernard (d. 1274), for example, suggested it to his fellow monks in his **Meditations on the Life of Christ.**

Hunt's argument that seeing an image of Jesus in the imagination is idolatry is an example of extreme Calvinism. Seeing Jesus either in picture or imagination is not idolatry for the obvious reason that Jesus is God, not a false idol of God.

His claim that the Jesus experienced in inner healing is a "spirit guide" is based on the experiences of a woman in his Christian Information Bureau who was into the occult. The woman performed an occult exercise of going into a trance state for the purpose of contacting a spirit guide. She found a spirit who claimed to be Jesus of Nazareth, but was in fact a demonic entity (Johanna Michaelsen, **The beautiful Side of Evil,** (Eugene, Oregon: Harvest House, 1982, page 75 ff.). To apply that extreme case, from an occult setting, to inner healing is another example of faulty reasoning: some spiritual experiences are proved to be demonic, therefore all spiritual experiences are demonic.

To agree with Hunt's assumptions and arguments and to submit to his fears would ultimately eliminate all forms of spiritual experiences from the life of the Christian.

William L. de Arteaga is an author and has been involved in the inner-healing ministry for the past 10 years in Atlanta, Georgia. His wife is assistant director of counseling at Mount Paran Church of God. They give inner-healing workshops.

*Reprinted by permission from **Ministries Magazine,** © by Strang Communications Company, Altamonte Springs, FL.

KOREAN LEADER:
IS HE A MYSTIC?*

By John Hurston

I do not have firsthand information about every topic **The Seduction of Christianity** treats but I do know about Paul Yonggi Cho.

I served as an Assemblies of God missionary for 34 years. I worked with Cho 17 years, first as a co-founding pastor and missionary advisor from 1958 to 1970, then as executive director of Church Growth International from 1976 to 1981.

When dealing with Cho's writings Hunt and McMahon have superimposed their own supposedly authoritative analysis of occultism upon selected teachings of a fine man of God.

They misrepresent Cho. Some examples are:

1. Cho does *not* say as the authors have stated that "miracles must all conform to his 'Law of the Fourth Dimension' " (page 101). He explains clearly that this analogy from the field of geometry helped him to understand and to explain to Bible students why miracles happened in occultish religions and gave him a means for explaining how the spirit world operates. Obviously Cho makes a clear distinction between the work of the Holy Spirit and the work of evil spirits.

2. It is not true, as the authors have said, that "Cho commends the Japanese Buddhist Soka-Gakkai for performing 'miracles,' " nor is it true that "he scolds Christians for not doing likewise" (page 102).

Cho does face the reality that the Soka-Gakkai, a relatively new religion in Japan, has millions of followers and does have miracles and healings. Cho states: "While Christianity has been in Japan for more than 100 years with only 0.5 percent of the population claiming to be Christian — there is only talk of theology and faith" (**The Fourth Dimension,** page 64). On the following two pages Cho warns: "Do not be deceived by talk of mind expansion, yoga, transcendental meditation, or Soka-Gakkai. They are developing the human fourth dimension, and in these cases are not in the good, but rather then evil fourth dimension."

Cho has a successful evangelistic and TV ministry in Japan with a vision to reach 10 million Japanese for Christ. He is having success in this ministry and has seen large numbers converted from Soka-Gakkai to Christianity. He is refuting Eastern mysticism in the best possible way.

Here are some statements made by Cho that point to his loyalty to New Testament teaching:

"I am as human as you are, and the only way I have salvation is through Jesus Christ" (page 88).

"The churches we build should be places where people get their solutions from the Lord" (page 99).

"The Holy Spirit can take Scripture...and apply it to a person's heart" (page 100).

"Never simply pick a promise out of God's Word and say, 'Oh, this is mine; I will repeat it over and over again. This is mine, this is mine!' NO!" (page 100).

"God gave His only begotten Son to be crucified on the cross so that this world could be saved and redeemed. That is God's uppermost goal — the redemption of souls!" (page 104).

"Through the Holy Spirit God puts in your heart the desire..." (page 108).

"The Holy Spirit will never contradict God's written Word" (page 111).

"...I meet God by reading the Scripture, the Word of God; and God's thoughts touch my thoughts in an unseen realm, and I have conversation with the Heavenly Father through the Word of God" (page 117).

This man of God leads a congregation of 500,000 and faithfully preaches biblical truth. These authors have attacked one of God's outstanding servants. The tacit insinuation that Cho is demonically influenced in what he said in **The Fourth Dimension** grieves me.

John Hurston is director of the pastoral staff at Word of Faith Family Church in Dallas, Texas. He served 34 years as a missionary for the Assemblies of God, including 17 years with Paul Yonggi Cho.

*Reprinted by permission from **Ministries Magazine,** ©1986 by Strang Communications, Altamonte Springs, FL.

HOW GOD USES VISION AND IMAGE

By Mark Virkler

The best approach to discovering what God has to say on a subject is to gather all the Scripture from Genesis to Revelation on that subject and then study through it several times, asking God to speak to you and recording the insights you receive. Using the word search option of CompuBIBLE, we have gathered on the following pages 383 verses that deal with dream, vision, seer, look, and eyes, along with occasional contextual verses that give clearer insight.

While asking God to grant you a spirit of revelation (Eph. 1:17,18) study these verses allowing God to reveal to you how He desires to use dream and vision in your life.

Following are some questions you may want to explore:

1. What is God's desired use of Dream and Vision in you life?
   a. does God Speak through them?
   b. how common should this experience be?
   c. does satan speak through dream and vision?
   d. how do we test dream and vision?
   e. Is there anything we are to do to promote the flow of Divine vision within us?

2. Does God use images as part of His encounter with us?
   a. If so, how is image to be used properly? Give some examples.
   b. What is the negative use of image? Give some examples.

3. Can we be trained in the use of the eyes of our hearts? Use Scripture to support you answer.

4. List other questions you may want to research also.

Index: **Vision (352 References)**
Title: *The place of dream and vision in one's spiritual life.*
Range: **GENESIS 1:1 to REVELATION 22:21**
Subject—
1. dream; 2. vision; 3. seer; 4. look; 5. eyes
The following verses related to dream and vision are broken into nine categories, to assist you in gleaning truths from each verse. The categories are:

1. The Divine Plan
2. Opened Eyes
3. The Place of Looking to See
4. The Title/Definition of Seer
5. Responsibilities of Seers
6. Examples of the Flow of Divine Vision
7. Interpretations Come From God
8. Testing Dream and Vision
9. The Inner Location of Visionary Experiences

The following verses are drawn from references to both dream and vision, since these words in Hebrew literature and in Scripture frequently are used interchangeably.

Category 1 — The Divine Plan

The declaration of God is that He intends to communicate Himself to man through the visionary capacity. After having proceeded in this manner throughout the entire Old Testament, he summarizes His work by saying that indeed He had spoken through multiplied visions (Hos. 12:10). He then continues by saying that He will do the same thing in the new covenant (Joel 2:8; and Acts 2:17). In the New Testament, he clearly reveals His plan to communicate to man through his visionary capacity by giving us the example of the life of Jesus, who is of course our perfect example of how to live (Jn. 5:19, 20; 8:38).

GEN. 3:5 For God doth know that in the day ye eat thereof, then your eyes shall be opened, and ye shall be as gods, knowing good and evil.

6 And when the woman saw that the tree (was) good for food, and that it (was) pleasant to the eyes, and a tree to be desired to make (one) wise, she took of the fruit thereof, and did eat, and gave unto her husband with her; and he did eat.

7 And the eyes of them both were opened, and they knew that they (were) naked; and they sewed fig leaves together, and made themselves aprons.

NUM 12:6 And he said, Hear now my words: if there be a prophet among you, (I) the Lord will make myself known unto him in a vision, (and) will speak unto him in a dream.

SAM 28:6 And when Saul inquired of the Lord, the Lord answered him not, neither by dreams, nor by Urim, not by prophets. And Samuel said to Saul. Why hast thou disquieted me, to bring me up? And Saul answered. I am sore distressed; for the Philistines make war against me, and God is departed from me, and answered me no more, neither by prophets, nor by dreams: therefore I have called thee that thou mayest make known unto me what I shall do.

PS. 89:19 Then thou spakest in vision to thy holy one, and saidst, I have laid help upon (one that is) mighty: I have exalted (one) chosen out of the people.

HOS. 12:10 I have also spoken by the prophets, and I have multiplied visions, and used similitudes, by the ministry of the prophets.

JOEL 2:28 And it shall come to pass afterward, (that) I will pour out my Spirit upon all flesh; and your sons and your daughters shall prophesy, your old men shall dream dreams, your young men shall see visions.

ACTS 2:17 And it shall come to pass in the last days, saith God, I will pour out of my Spirit upon all flesh; and your sons and your daughters shall prophesy, and your young men shall see visions, and your old men shall dream dreams.

JOHN 5:19 Then answered Jesus and said unto them, verily, verily I say unto you, the Son can do nothing of himself, but what he seeth the Father do: for whatsoever things he doeth, these also doeth the Son likewise.
    20 For the Father loveth the son and showeth him all things that himself doeth: and he will show him greater works than these, that ye may marvel.

JOHN 8:38 I speak that which I have seen with my Father: and ye do that which ye have seen with your father.

Category 2 — Opened Eyes

These verses demonstrate that there is a place and a need for us to have the eyes of our heart opened, so we can see the vision of God. The Scripture clearly states that not everyone has opened eyes. We must recognize this lack and need, and seek God that He would open the eyes of our hearts.

GEN 21:19   And God opened her eyes, and she saw a well of water; and she went, and filled the bottle with water, and gave the lad drink.

NUM 22:31   Then the Lord opened the eyes of Balaam, and he saw the angel of the Lord standing in the way, and his sword drawn in his hand: and he bowed down his head, and fell flat on his face.

NUM 24:2   And Balaam lifted up his eyes, and he saw Israel abiding (in his tents) according to their tribes: and the spirit of God came upon him.
   3   And he took up his parable, and said, Balaam the son of Beor hath said, and the man whose eyes are open hath said:
   4   He hath said, which heard the words of God, which saw the vision of the Almighty, (falling into a trance), but having his eyes open:
   15   And he took up his parable, and said, Balaam the sons of Beor hath said, and the man whose eyes are open hath said.
   16   He hath said, which heard the words of God, and knew the knowledge of the most High, (which) saw the vision of the Almighty, falling (into a trance), but having his eyes open:

DEUT 29:2   And Moses called unto all Israel, and said unto them, Ye have seen all that the Lord did before your eyes in the land of Egypt unto Pharaoh, and unto all his servants, and unto all his land:
   3   The great temptations which their eyes have seen, the signs, and those great miracles.
   4   Yet the Lord hath not given you a heart to perceive, and eyes to see, and ears to hear unto this day.

1 SAM 3:1   Now the boy Samuel was ministering to the Lord before Eli. And word from the Lord was rare in those days, visions were infrequent.
   2   And it came to pass at that time, when Eli (was) laid down in his place, and his eyes began to wax dim, (that) he could not see:
   3   And ere the lamp of God went out in the temple of the Lord, where the ark of God (was), and Samuel was laid down (to sleep);
   4   That the Lord called Samuel: and he answered, Here (am) I.
   5   And he ran unto Eli, and said, Here (am) I; for thou callst me. And he said, I called not; lie down again. And he went and lay down.
   6   And the Lord called yet again, Samuel. And Samuel arose and went to Eli, and said, Here (am) I; for thou didst call me. And he answered, I called not, my son; lie down again.

7 Now Samuel did not yet know the Lord, neither was the word of the Lord yet revealed unto him.

8 And the Lord called Samuel again the third time. And he arose and went to Eli, and said, Here (am) I; for thou didst call me. And Eli perceived that the Lord had called the child.

9 Therefore Eli said unto Samuel, Go, lie down; and it shall be, if he call thee, that thou shalt say, Speak, Lord; for thy servant heareth. So Samuel went and lay down in his place.

10 And the Lord came, and stood, and called as at other times, Samuel, Samuel. Then Samuel answered, Speak; for thy servant hearth.

15 And Samuel lay until the morning, and opened the doors of the house of the Lord. And Samuel feared to shew Eli the vision.

2 KINGS 6:15 And when the servant of the man was risen early, and gone forth, behold, an host compassed the city both with horses and chariots. And his servant said unto him, Alas, my master, how shall we do?

16 And he answered, Fear not: for they that be with us are more than those that be with them.

17 And Elisha prayed, and said, Lord, I pray thee, open his eyes, that he may see. And the Lord opened the eyes of the young man; and he saw; and behold, the mountain (was) full of horses and chariots of fire round about Elisha.

JOB 33:15 In a dream, in a vision of the night, when deep sleep falleth upon men, in slumberings upon the bed;

16 Then he openeth the ears of men, and sealeth their instruction.

PS. 119:18 Open thou mine eyes, that I may behold wondrous things out of thy law.

ISA. 42:18 Hear, ye deaf; and look, ye blind, that ye may see.

19 Who (is) blind, but my servant? Or deaf, as my messenger (that) I sent? Who (is) blind as (he that is) perfect, and blind and the Lord's servant?

20 Seeing many things, but thou observest not; opening the ears, but he heareth not.

ISA. 44:18 They have not known nor understood: for he hath shut their eyes, that they cannot see; (and) their hearts, that they cannot understand.

JER. 5:21 Hear now this. O foolish people, and without understanding, which have eyes, and see not; which have ears, and hear not:

LAM. 2:9 Her gates are sunk into the ground; he hath destroyed and broken her bars; her king and her princes (are) among the Gentiles: the law (is) no (more): her prophets also find no vision from the Lord.

MATT. 13:15 For this people's heart is waxed gross, and (their) ears are dull of hearing, and their eyes they have closed; lest at any time they should see with (their) eyes, and hear with their ears, and should understand with (their) heart, and should be converted, and I should heal them.
16 But blessed (are) your eyes, for they see; and your ears, for they hear.

MARK 8:18 Having eyes, see ye not? And having ears, hear ye not? And do ye not remember?

JOHN 12:40 He hath blinded their eyes, and hardened their heart; that they should not see with (their) eyes, not understand with (their) heart, and be converted, and I should heal them.

ACTS 28:27 For the heart of this people is waxed gross, and their ears are dull of hearing, and their eyes have they closed; lest they should see with (their) eyes, and hear with (their) ears, and understand with (their) ears, and should be converted, and I should heal them.

ROM. 11:8 (According as it is written, God hath given them the spirit of slumber, eyes that they should not see, and ears that they should not hear); unto this day.
10 Let their eyes be darkened, that they may not see, and bow down their back alway.

2 COR. 4:18 While we look not at the things which are seen, but at the things which are not seen: for the things which are seen (are) temporal; but the things which are not seen (are) eternal.

Category 3 — The Place of Looking to See

I had never fully recognized the emphasis Scripture places on lifting up our eyes and looking to see until I did this study and noted the host of verses that support this truth. In surveying groups of people, I have found that only about one-to-two percent of evangelical Christians have heard a sermon instructing them on the place and priority of looking into the spirit world to see the vision of Almighty God. In light of the vast scriptural support of this truth, it is high time we begin preaching on it.

GEN. 18:1 And the Lord appeared unto him in the plains of Mamre: and he sat in the tent door in the heat of the day:

2 And he lift up his eyes and looked, and, lo, three men stood by him: and when he saw (them), he ran to meet them from the tent door, and bowed himself toward the ground.

GEN. 31:10 And it came to pass at the time that the cattle conceived, that I lifted up mine eyes, and saw in a dream, and, behold, the rams which leaped upon the cattle (were) ringstraked, speckled, and grisled.

11 And the angel of God spake unto me in a dream, (saying), Jacob:
And I said, Here (am) I.

12 And he said, Lift up now thine eyes, and see, all the rams which leap upon the cattle (are) ringstraked, speckled, and grisled: for I have seen all that Laban doeth unto thee.

EXOD. 3:1 Now Moses kept the flock of Jethro his father-in-law, the priest of Midian: and he led the flock to the backside of the desert, and came to the mountain of God, (even) to Horeb.

2 And the angel of the Lord appeared unto him in a flame of fire fire out of the midst of a bush: and he looked, and, behold, the bush burned with fire, and the bush was (not) consumed.

3 And Moses said, I will now turn aside, and see this great sight, why the bush is not burnt.

4 And when the Lord saw that he turned aside to see, God called unto him out of the midst of the bush, and said, Moses, Moses. And he said, Here (am) I.

5 And he said, Draw not nigh hither: put off thy shoes from off thy feet, for the place whereon thou standest (is) (holy) ground.

6 Moreover he said, I (am) the God of thy father, the God of Abraham, the God of Isaac, and the God of Jacob. And Moses hid his face: for he was afraid to look upon God.

EXOD. 16:9 And Moses spake unto Aaron, Say unto all the congregation of the children of Israel, Come near before the Lord: for he hath heard your murmurings.

10 And it came to pass, as Aaron spake unto the whole congregation of the children of Israel, that they looked toward the wilderness, and, behold, the glory of the Lord appeared in the cloud.

JOSH. 5:13 And it came to pass, when Joshua was by Jericho, that he lifted up his eyes and looked, and, behold, there stood a man over against him with his sword drawn in his hand: and Joshua went unto him, and said unto him (Art) thou for us, or for our adversaries?

14 And he said, Nay; but (as) captain of the host of the Lord am I now come. And Joshua fell on his face to the earth, and did worship, and said unto him, What saith my lord unto his servant?

15 And the captain of the Lord's host said unto Joshua, Loose thy shoe from off thy foot; for the place whereon thou standest (is) holy. And Joshua did so.

1 CHRON. 21:16 And David lifted up his eyes, and saw the angel of the Lord stand between the earth and the heaven, having a drawn sword in his hand stretched out over Jerusalem. Then David and the elders (of Israel, who were) clothed in sackcloth, fell upon their faces.

DAN. 10:1 In the third year of Cyrus King of Persia a thing was revealed unto Daniel, whose name was called Belteshazzar; and that king (was) true, but the time appointed (was) long: and he understood the thing, and had understanding of the vision.

5 *Then I lifted up mine eyes,* and looked, and behold a certain man clothed in linen, whose loins (were) girded with fine gold of Uphaz.

6 His body also (was) like the Beryl, and his face as the appearance of lightning, and his eyes as lamps of fire, and his arms and his feet like in colour to polished brass, and the voice of his words like the voice of a multitude.

7 *And I Daniel alone saw the vision:* for the men that were with me saw not the vision; but a great quaking fell upon them, so that they fled to hide themselves.

8 Therefore I was left alone, and saw this great vision, and there remained no strength in me: for my comeliness was turned in me into corruption, and I retained no strength.

9 Yet heard I the voice of his words: and when I heard the voice of his words, then I was in a deep sleep on my face, and my face toward the ground.

10 And, behold, a hand touched me, which set me upon my knees and (upon) the palms of my hands.

11 And he said unto me, O Daniel, a man greatly beloved, understand the words that I speak unto thee, and stand upright: for unto thee am I now sent. And when he had spoken this word unto me, I stood trembling.

12 Then said he unto me, Fear not, Daniel: for from the first day that thou didst set thine heart to understand, and to chasten thyself before thy God, thy words were heard, and I am come for thy words.

13 But the prince of the kingdom of Persia withstood me one and twenty days: but, lo, Michael, one of the chief princes came to help me; and I remained there with the kings of Persia.

14 Now I can come to make thee understand what shall befall

thy people in the latter days: for yet the vision (is) for (many) days.

15 And when he had spoken such words unto me, I set my face toward the ground, and I became dumb.

16 And, behold, (one) like the similitude of the sons of men touched my lips: then I opened my mouth, and spake, and said unto him that stood before me, O my lord, by the vision my sorrows are turned upon me, and I have retained no strength.

PS. 5:3 My voice shalt thou hear in the morning, O Lord; in the morning will I direct (my prayer) unto thee, and will look up.

PS. 25:15 Mine eyes (are) ever toward the Lord; for he shall pluck my feet out of the net.

PS. 123:1 Unto thee lift I up mine eyes, O thou that dwellest in the heavens.

2 Behold, as the eyes of servants (look) unto the hand of their masters, (and) as the eyes of a maiden unto the hand of her mistress; so our eyes (wait) upon the Lord our God, until that he have mercy upon us.

PS 141:8 But mine eyes (are) unto thee, O God the Lord: in thee is my trust; leave not my soul destitute.

ISA. 8:17 And I will wait upon the Lord, that hideth his face from the house of Jacob, and I will look for him.

ISA. 17:7 At that day shall a man look to his Maker, and his eyes shall have respect to the Holy One of Israel.

8 And he shall not look to the altars, the work of his hands, neither shall respect (that) which his fingers have made, either the groves, or the images.

ISA. 40:26 Lift up your eyes on high, and behold who hath created these (things), that bringeth out their host by number: he calleth them all by names by the greatness of his might, for that (he is) strong in power; not one faileth.

EZEK. 1:1 Now it came to pass in the thirtieth year, in the fourth (month), in the fifth (day) of the month, as I (was) among the captives by the river of Chebar, (that) the heavens were opened, and I saw visions of God.

4 And I looked, and, behold, a whirlwind came out of the north, a great cloud, and a fire unfolding itself, and a brightness (was) about it,

and out of the midst thereof as the colour of amber, out of the midst of the fire.

EZEK. 2:9 And when I looked, behold, a hand (was) sent unto me; and, lo, a roll of a book (was) therein;

EZEK. 8:3 And he put forth the form of a hand, and took me by a lock of mine head; and the spirit lifted me up between the earth and the heaven, and brought me in the visions of God to Jerusalem, to the door of the inner gate that looketh toward the north; where (was) the seat of the image of jealousy, which provoketh to jealousy.

4 And, behold, the glory of the God of Israel (was) there, according to the vision that I saw in the plain.

5 Then said he unto me, Son of man, lift up thine eyes now the way toward the north. So I lifted up mine eyes the way toward the north, and behold northward at the gate of the altar this image of jealousy in the entry.

7 And he brought me to the door of the court; and when I looked, behold a hole in the wall.

EZEK. 10:1 Then I looked, and, behold, in the firmament that was above the head of the cherubims there appeared over them as it were a sapphire stone, as the appearance of the likeness of a throne.

9 And when I looked behind the four wheels by the cherubims, one wheel by one cherub, and another wheel by another cherub; and the appearance of the wheels (was) as the colour of a beryl stone.

EZEK. 44:1 Then he brought me back the way of the gate of the outward sanctuary which looketh toward the east; and it (was) shut.

4 Then brought he me the way of the north gate before the house; and I looked, and, behold, the glory of the Lord filled the house of the Lord; and I fell upon my face.

5 And the Lord said unto me, Son of man, mark well, and behold with thine eyes, and hear with thine ears all that I say unto thee concerning all the ordinances of the house of the Lord, and all the laws thereof; and mark well the entering in of the house, with every going forth of the sanctuary.

DAN. 12:5 Then I Daniel looked, and, behold, there stood other two, the one on this side of the bank of the river, and the other on that side of the bank of the river.

ZECH. 1:18 Then lifted up mine eyes, and saw, and behold four horns.

ZECH. 2:1 I lifted up mine eyes again, and looked, and behold a man with a measuring line in his hand.

ZECH 4:2 And said unto me, What seest thou? And I said, I have looked, And behold a candlestick all (of) gold, with a bowl upon the top of it, and his seven lamps thereon, and seven pipes to the seven lamps, which (are) upon the top thereof:

ZECH. 5:1 Then I turned, and lifted up mine eyes, and looked, and behold a flying roll.

ZECH. 5:5 Then the angel that talked with me went forth, and said unto me, Lift up now thine eyes, and see what (is) this that goeth forth.

ZECH. 5:9 Then lifted I up mine eyes, and looked, and, behold, there came out two women, and the wind (was) in their wings for they had wings like the wings of a stork: and they lifted up the ephah between the earth and the heaven.

ZECH. 6:1 And I turned, and lifted up mine eyes, and looked, and, behold, there came four chariots out from between two mountains; and the mountains (were) mountains of brass.

ACTS 7:55 But he, being full of the Holy Ghost, looked up stedfastly into heaven, and saw the glory of God, and Jesus standing on the right hand of God.

REV. 4:1 After this I looked, and, behold, a door (was) opened in heaven: and the first voice which I heard (was) as it were of a trumpet talking with me; which said, Come up hither, and I will shew thee things which must be hereafter.

REV. 6:8 And I looked, and behold a pale horse: and his name that sat on him was Death, and Hell followed with him. And power was given unto them over the fourth part of the earth, to kill with sword, and with hunger, and with death, and with the beasts of the earth.

REV. 14:1 And I looked, and, lo, a Lamb stood on the mount Sion, and with him an hundred forty (and) four thousand, having his Father's name written in their foreheads.

REV. 14:14 And I looked, and behold a white cloud, and upon the cloud (one) sat like unto the Son of man, having on his head a golden crown, and in his hand a sharp sickle.

REV. 15:5 And after that I looked, and, behold, the temple of the tabernacle of the testimony in heaven was opened.

Category 4 — The Title/Definition of Seer

Prophets were also called seers. They were people who saw in the spirit world the vision of Almighty God. This was a common title and office in Scripture and needs to be restored to the life of the church. We need to again train up prophets who are seers, those who can see into the spirit world. Actually, in the New Covenant the veil has been torn, and now we **all** have access directly before the throne - room of Almighty God. We all may prophesy (I Cor. 14:31).

1 SAM 9:9 (Beforetime in Israel, when a man went to inquire of God, thus he spake, Come, and let us go to the seer: for (he that is) now (call-ed a Prophet was beforetime called a Seer).

    10 Then said Saul to his servant, Well said; come, let us go. So they went unto the city where the man of God (was).

    11 (And) as they went up the hill to the city, they found young maidens going out to draw water, and said unto them, is the seer here?

2 Sam. 24:11	Gad	David's seer
1 Chron. 25:5	Heman	the king's seer
1 Chron. 29:29	Samuel	the seer
2 Chron. 9:29	Iddo	the seer
2 Chron. 19:2	Hanani	the seer
2 Chron. 29:30	Asaph	the seer
2 Chron. 35:15	Juduthum	the king's seer
2 Sam. 15:27	Zadioc	a seer
Amos 7:12	Amos	thou seer

Category 5 — Responsibilities of Seers

In the following verses you will observe a number of the responsibilities of a seer. They included consulting and advising kings, exhorting the people, delivering the word of God to the people, and recording the word of God.

2 SAM. 24:11 For when David was up in the morning, the Word of the Lord came unto the prophet Gad, David's seer, saying,

    12 Go and say unto David, Thus saith the Lord, I offer thee three (things); choose thee one of them, that I may (do it) unto thee.

2 KINGS 17:13 Yet the Lord testified against Israel, and against Judah, by all the prophets, (and by) all the seers, saying, Turn ye from your evil ways, and keep my commandments (and) my statutes, according to all the law which I commanded your fathers, and which I sent to you by my servants the prophets.

1 CHRON. 9:22 All these (which were) chosen to be porters in the gates (were) two hundred and twelve. These were reckoned by their gene-alogy in their villages, whom David and Samuel the seer did ordain in their set office.

1 CHRON. 12:3 And it came to pass the same night, that the word of God came to Nathan, saying,
     4 Go and tell David my servant, Thus saith the Lord, Thou shalt not build me an house to dwell in:
     15 According to all these words, and according to all this vision, so did Nathan speak unto David.

1 CHRON. 21:9 And the Lord spake unto Gad, David's seer, saying,
     10 Go and tell David, saying, Thus saith the Lord, I offer thee three (things): choose thee one of them, that I may do (it) unto thee.

1 CHRON. 26:28 And all that Samuel the seer, and Saul the son of Kish, and Abner the son of Ner, and Joab the son of Zeruiah, had dedi-cated; (and) whosoever had dedicated (anything, it was) under the hand of Shelomith, and of his brethren.

1 CHRON. 29:29 Now the acts of David the king, first and last, behold, they (are) written in the book of Samuel the seer, and in the book of Nathan the prophet, and in the book of Gad the seer.

2 CHRON. 9:29 Now the rest of the acts of Solomon, first and last, (are) they not written in the book of Nathan the prophet, and in the prophecy of Ahijah the Shilonite, and in the visions of Iddo the seer against Jeroboam the son of Nebat?

2 CHRON. 12:15 Now the acts of Rehoboam, first and last, (are) they not written in the book of Shemaiah the prophet, and of Iddo the seer concerning genealogies? And (there were) wars between Rehoboam and Jeroboam continually.

2 CHRON. 16:7 And at that time Hanani the seer came to Asa king of Judah, and said unto him, Because thou hast relied on the king of Syria,

and not relied on the Lord thy God, therefore is the host of the king of Syria escaped out of thine hand.

8 Were not the Ethiopians and the Lubims a huge host, with very many chariots and horsemen? Yet, because thou didst rely on the Lord, he delivered them into thine hand.

9 For the eyes of the Lord run to and fro throughout the whole earth, to shew himself strong in the behalf of (them) whose heart (is) perfect toward him. Herein thou hast done foolishly: therefore from henceforth thou shalt have wars.

10 Then Asa was wroth with the seer, and put him in a prison house; for (he was) in a rage with him because of this (thing). And Asa oppressed (some) of the people the same time.

2 CHRON. 29:25 And he set the Levites in the house of the Lord with cymbals, with psalteries, and with harps, according to the commandment of David, and of Gad the king's seer, and Nathan the prophet: for (so was) the commandment of the Lord by his prophets.

2 CHRON. 32:32 Now the rest of the acts of Hezekiah, and his goodness, behold, they (are) written in the vision of Isaiah the prophet, the son of Amoz, (and) in the book of the kings of Judah and Israel.

2 CHRON. 33:18 Now the rest of the acts of Manasseh, and his prayer unto his God, and the words of the seers that spake to him in the name of the Lord God of Israel, behold, they (are written) in the book of the kings of Israel.

19 His prayer also, and (how God) was intreated of him, and all his sin, and his trespass, and the places wherein he built high places, and set up groves and graven images, before he was humbled: behold, they (are) written among the sayings of the seers.

2 CHRON. 35:15 And the singers the sons of Asaph (were) in their place, according to the commandment of David, and Asaph, and Heman, and Jeduthun the king's seer; and the porters (waited) at every gate; they might not depart from their service; for their brethren the Levites prepared for them.

EZEK. 40:2 In the visions of God brought he me into the land of Israel, and set me upon a very high mountain, by which (was) as the frame of a city on the south.

4 And the man said unto me, Son of man, behold with thine eyes, and hear with thine ears, and set thine heart upon all that I shall shew thee; for to the intent that I might shew (them) unto thee (art) though brought hither: declare all that thou seest to the house of Israel.

6 Then came he unto the gate which looketh toward the east, and went up the stairs thereof, and measured the threshold of the gate (which was) one reed broad; and the other threshold (of the gate, which was) one reed broad.

HAB. 2:2 And the Lord answered me, and said, Write the vision, and make (it) plain upon tables, that he may run that readeth it.
3 For the vision (is) yet for an appointed time, but at the end it shall speak, and not lie: though it tarry, wait for it; because it will surely come, it will not tarry.

REV. 1:10 I was in the Spirit on the Lord's day, and heard behind me a great voice, as of a trumpet.
11 Saying, I am Alpha and Omega, the first and the last: and what thou seest, write in above.
14 His head and (his) hairs (were) white like wool, as white as snow; and his eyes (were) as a flame of fire:

Category 6 — Examples of the Flow of Divine Vision

In the following verses you will find many kinds of messages God gives as He fills man's visionary capacity with His divine vision. Communicating through dream and vision, God warns, instructs, rebukes, comforts, encourages, enlightens, fortells future events, imparts divine gifts, and sets people aside for the ministry. Note these and others as you read through the following verses.

GEN 15:1 After these things the word of the Lord came unto Abram in a vision, saying, Fear not, Abram: I (am) thy shield, (and) the exceeding great reward.

GEN 20:3 But God came to Abimelech in a dream by night, and said to him, Behold thou (art but) a dead man, for the woman which thou hast taken; for she (is) a man's wife.
6 And God said unto him in a dream, Yea, I know that thou didst this in the integrity of thy heart; for I also withheld thee from sinning against me; therefore suffered I thee not to touch her.

GEN 28:12 And he dreamed, and behold a ladder set up on the earth, and the top of it reached to heaven: and behold the angels of God ascending and descending on it.

GEN 31:24 And God came to Laban the Syrian in a dream by night, and said unto him, Take heed that thou speak not to Jacob either good or bad.

APP. A 2

GEN 37:5 And Joseph dreamed a dream, and he told (it) his brethren: and they hated him yet the more.

6 And he said unto them, Hear, I pray you, this dream which I have dreamed:

8 And his brethren said to him, Shalt thou indeed reign over us? or shalt thou indeed have dominion over us? And they hated him yet the more for his dreams, and for his words.

9 And he dreamed yet another dream, and told it his brethren, and said, Behold, I have dreamed a dream more; and, behold, the sun and the moon and the eleven stars made obeisance to me.

10 And he told (it) to his father, and to his brethren: and his father rebuked him, and said unto him, What (is) this dream that thou hast dreamed? Shall I and thy mother and thy brethren indeed come to bow done ourselves to thee to the earth?

GEN 41:1 And it came to pass at the end of two full years, that Pharaoh dreamed.

5 And he slept and dreamed the second time: and, behold, seven ears of corn came up upon one stalk, rank and good.

7 And the seven thin ears devoured the seven rank and full ears. And Pharaoh awoke, and, behold, (it was) a dream.

8 And it came to pass in the morning that his spirit was troubled; and he sent and called for all the magicians of Egypt, and all the wise men thereof: and Pharaoh told them his dream; but (there was) none that could interpret them unto Pharaoh.

11 And we dreamed a dream in one night, I and he; we dreamed each man according to the interpretation of his dream.

12 And (there was) there with us a young man, a Hebrew, servant to the captain of the guard; and we told him, and he interpreted to us our dreams; to each man according to his dream he did interpret.

15 And Pharaoh said unto Joseph, I have dreamed a dream, and (there is) none that can interpret it: and I have heard say of thee, (that) thou canst understand a dream to interpret it.

17 And Pharaoh said unto Joseph, In my dream, behold, I stood upon the bank of the river.

22 And I saw in my dream, and, behold, seven ears came up in one stalk, full and good:

25 And Joseph said unto Pharaoh, The dream of Pharaoh (is) one: God hath shewed Pharaoh what he (is) about to do.

26 The seven good kine (are) seven years; and the seven good ears (are) seven years: the dream (is) one.

32 And for that the dream was doubled unto Pharaoh twice; (it is)

because the thing (is) established by God, and God will shortly bring it to pass.

GEN 46:2 And God spake unto Israel in the visions of the night and said, Jacob, And he said, Here (am) I.
3 And he said, I am God, the God of thy father: fear not to go down into Egypt; for I will there make of thee a great nation:
4 I will go down with thee into Egypt; and I will also surely bring thee up (again); and Joseph shall put his hand upon thine eyes.

JDG 7:13 And when Gideon was come, behold, (there was) a man that told a dream unto his fellow, and said, Behold, I dreamed a dream, and, lo, a cake of barley bread tumbled into the host of Midian, and came unto a test, and smote it that it fell, and overturned it, that the tent lay along.
14 And his fellow answered and said, This (is) nothing else save the sword of Gideon the son of Joash, a man of Israel: (for) into his hand hath God delivered Midian, and all the host.
15 And it was (so), when Gideon heard the telling of the dream, and the interpretation thereof, that he worshipped, and returned into the host of Israel, and said, Arise; for the Lord hath delivered into your hand the host of Midian.

2 SAM 7:4 And it came to pass that night, that the word of the Lord came unto Nathan, saying,
5 God and tell my servant David, Thus saith the Lord, Shalt thou build me a house for me to dwell in?
6 Whereas I have not dwelt in (any) house since the time that I brought up the children of Israel out of Egypt, even to this day, but have walked in a tent and in a tabernacle.
7 In all (the places) wherein I have walked with all the children of Israel spake I a word with any of the tribes of Israel, whom I commanded to feed my people Israel, saying, Why build ye not me a house of cedar?
8 Now therefore so shalt thou say unto my servant David, Thus saith the Lord of hosts, I took thee from the sheepcote, from following the sheep, to be ruler over my people, over Israel:
9 And I was with thee whithersoever thou wentest, and have cut off thine enemies out of thy sight and have made thee a great name, like unto the name of the great (men) that (are) in the earth.
10 Moreover I will appoint a place for my people Israel, and will plant them, that they may dwell in a place of their own, and move no more; neither shall the children of wickedness afflict them any more, as beforetime.

17 According to all these words, and according to all this vision, so did Nathan speak unto David.

1 KINGS 3:5 In Gideon the Lord appeared to Solomon in a dream by night: and God said, Ask what I shall give thee.

6 And Solomon said, Thou hast shewed unto thy servant David my father great mercy, according as he walked before thee in truth, and thou hast kept for him this great kindness, that thou hast given him a son to sit on his thorne, as (it is) this day.

7 And now, O Lord my God, thou hast made thy servant king instead of David my father: and I (am but) a little child: I know not (how) to go out or come in.

8 And thy servant (is) in the midst of thy people which thou hast chosen, a great people, that cannot be numbered nor counted for multitude.

9 Give therefore thy servant an understanding heart to judge thy people, that I may discern between good and bad: for who is able to judge this thy so great a people?

10 And the speech pleased the Lord, that Solomon had asked this thing.

11 And God said unto him, Because thou hast asked this thing, and hast not asked for thyself long life, neither hast asked riches for thyself, nor hast asked the life of thine enemies; but hast asked for thyself understanding to discern judgment;

12 Behold, I have done according to thy words: lo, I have given thee a wise and an understanding heart; so that there was none like thee before thee, neither after thee shall any arise like unto thee.

13 And I have also given thee that which thou hast not asked, both riches, and honour: so that there shall not be any among the kings like unto thee all thy days.

14 And if thou wilt walk in my ways, to keep my statutes, and my commandments, as thy father David did walk, then I will lengthen thy days.

15 And Solomon awoke; and behold, (it was) a dream. And he came to Jerusalem, and stood before the ark of the covenant of the Lord, and offered up burnt offerings, and offered peace offerings, and made a feast to all his servants.

PROV. 29:18 Where (there is) no vision, the people perish: but he that keepeth the law, happy (is) he.

ISA. 1:1 The vision of Isaiah the son of Amoz, which he saw concerning Judah and Jerusalem in the days of Uzziah, Jotham, Ahaz, (and) Hezekiah, kings of Judah.

ISA. 6:1 In the year that king Uzziah died I saw also the Lord sitting upon a throne, high and lifted up, and his train filled the temple.

2 Above it stood the seraphims: each one had six wings: with twain he covered his face, and with twain he covered his feet, and with twain he did fly.

3 And one cried unto another, and said, Holy, holy, holy, (is) the Lord of hosts: the whole earth (is) full of his glory.

4 And the posts of the door moved at the voice of him that cried, and the house was filled with smoke.

5 Then said I, Woe (is) me! for I am undone; because I (am) a man of unclean lips, and I dwell in the midst of a people of unclean lips for mine eyes have seen the King, 'the Lord of hosts.

6 Then flew one of the seraphims unto me, having a live coal in his hand, (which) he had taken with the tongs from off the altar:

7 And he laid (it) upon my mouth, and said, Lo, this hath touched thy lips; and thine iniquity is taken away, and thy sin purged.

8 Also I heard the voice of the Lord, saying, Whom shall I send, and who will go for us? Then said I, Here (am) I; send me.

9 And he said, Go, and tell this people, Hear ye indeed, but understand not; and see ye indeed, but perceive not.

10 Make the heart of this people fat, and make their ears heavy, and shut their eyes; lest they see with their eyes, and hear with their ears, and understand with their heart, and convert, and be healed.

EZEK. 11:1 Moreover the spirit lifted me up, and brought me unto the east gate of the Lord's house, which looketh eastward: and behold at the door of the gate five and twenty men; among whom I saw Jaazaniah the son of Azur, and Pelatiah the son of Benaiah, princes of the people.

EZEK. 11:24 Afterwards the spirit took me up, and brought me in a vision by the Spirit of God into Chaldea, to them of the captivity. So the vision that I had seen went up from me.

EZEK. 43:1 Afterwards he brought me to the gate, (even) the gate that looketh toward the east:

2 And, behold, the glory of the God of Israel came from the way of the east; and his voice (was) like a noise of many waters: and the earth shined with his glory.

3 And (it was) according to the appearance of the vision which I saw, (even) according to the vision that I saw when I came to destroy the city: and the visions (were) like the vision that I saw by the river Chebar; and I fell upon my face.

4 And the glory of the Lord came into the house by the way of

the gate whose prospect (is) toward the east.

5 So the spirit took me up, and brought me into the inner court; and, behold, the glory of the Lord filled the house.

6 And I heard (him) speaking unto me out of the house; and the man stood by me.

DAN. 2:1 And in the second year of the reign of Nebuchadnezzar, Nebuchadnezzar dreamed dreams, wherewith his spirit was troubled, and his sleep brake from him.

2 Then the king commanded to call the magicians, and the astrologers, and the sorcerers, and the Chaldeans, for to shew the king his dreams. So they came and stood before the king.

3 And the king said unto them, I have dreamed a dream, and my spirit was troubled to know the dream.

4 Then spake the Chaldeans to the king in Syriack, O king, live forever: tell thy servants the dream, and we will shew the interpretation.

5 The king answered and said to the Chaldeans, The thing is gone from me: if ye will not make known unto me the dream, with the interpretation thereof, ye shall be cut in pieces, and your houses shall be made a dunghill.

6 But if ye shew the dream, and the interpretation thereof, ye shall receive of me gifts and rewards and great honour: therefore shew me the dream, and the interpretation thereof.

7 They answered again and said, Let the king tell his servants the dream, and we will shew the interpretation of it.

8 The king answered and said, I know of certainty that ye would gain the time, because ye see the thing is gone from me.

9 But if ye will not make known unto me the dream, (there is but) one decree for you: for ye have prepared lying and corrupt words to speak before me, till the time be changed: therefore tell me the dream, and I shall know that ye can shew me the interpretation thereof.

19 Then was the secret revealed unto Daniel in a night vision. Then Daniel blessed the God of heaven.

26 The king answered and said to Daniel, vhose name (was) Belteshazzar, Art thou able to make known unto me the dream which I have seen, and the interpretation thereof?

28 But there is a God in heaven that revealeth secrets, and maketh known to the king Nebuchadnezzar what shall be in the latter days. Thy dream, and the vision of thy head upon thy bed, are these:

36 This (is) the dream; and we will tell the interpretation thereof before the king.

OBAD. 1:1 The vision of Obadiah. Thus saith the Lord God concerning Edom; We have heard a rumour from the Lord, and an ambassador is

sent among the heathen, Arise ye, and let us rise up against her in battle.

NAH. 1:1 The burden of Ninevah. The book of the vision of Nahum the
Elkoshite.

MATT. 1:20 But while he thought on these things, behold, the angel of
the Lord appeared unto him in a dream, saying, Joseph, thou son of
David, fear not to take unto thee Mary thy wife: for that which is conceived in her is of the Holy Ghost.

MATT. 2:12 And being warned of God in a dream that they should not
return to Herod, they departed into their own country another way.
    13 And when they were departed, behold, the angel of the Lord
appeareth to Joseph in a dream, saying, Arise, and take the young child
and his mother, and flee into Egypt, and be thou there until I bring thee
word: for Herod will seek the young child to destroy him.

MATT. 2:19 But when Herod was dead, behold, an angel of the Lord
appeareth in a dream to Joseph in Egypt.
    20 Saying, Arise and take the young child and his mother and go
into the land of Israel: for they are dead which sought the young child's
life.
    21 And he arose and took the young child and his mother, and
came into the land of Israel.
    22 But when he heard that Archelaus did reign in Judea in the
room of his father Herod, he was afraid to go thither: notwithstanding,
being warned of God in a dream, he turned aside into the parts of
Galilee:

LUKE 24:22 Yea, and certain women of an company made us astonished, which were early at the sepulchre.
    23 And when they found not his body, they came, saying, that
they had also seen a vision of angels, which said that he was alive.

ACTS 9:10 And there was a certain disciple at Damascus, named
Ananias; and to him said the Lord in a vision, Ananias, and he said,
Behold, I (am here), Lord.
    11 And the Lord (said) unto him, Arise, and go into the street
which is called Straight, and inquire in the house of Judas for (one)
called Saul, of Tarsus: for, behold, he prayeth.
    12 And hath seen in a vision a man named Ananias coming in,
and putting (his) hand on him, that he might receive his sight.

ACTS 10:3 He saw in a vision evidently about the ninth hour of the day an angel of God coming in to him, and saying unto him, Cornelius.

4 And when he looked on him, he was afraid, and said, What is it, Lord? And he said unto him, Thy prayers and thine alms are come up for a memorial before God.

5 And now send men to Joppa, and call for one Simon, whose surname is Peter.

ACTS 10:10 . . .While they made ready, he fell into a trance,

11 And saw heaven opened. . .

17 Now while Peter doubted in himself what this vision which he had seen should mean, behold, the men which were sent from Cornelius had made inquiry for Simon's house, and stood before the gate,

18 And called, and asked whether Simon, which was surnamed Peter, were lodged there.

19 While Peter thought on the vision, the Spirit said unto him, Behold, three men seek thee.

34 Then Peter opened his mouth and said, of a truth I perceive that God is no respecter of persons.

ACTS 16:9 And a vision appeared to Paul in the night; There stood a man of Macedonia, and prayed him, saying, Come over into Macedonia, and help us.

10 And after he had seen the vision, immediately we endeavoured to go into Macedonia, assuredly gathering that the Lord had called us for to preach the gospel unto them.

ACTS 18:9 Then spake the Lord to Paul in the night by a vision, Be not afraid, but speak, and hold not thy peace:

ACTS 26:12 Whereupon as I went to Damascus with authority and commission from the chief priests.

13 At midday, O king, I saw in the way a light from heaven, above the brightness of the sun, shining round about me and them which journeyed with me.

14 And when we were all fallen to the earth, I heard a voice speaking unto me, and saying in the Hebrew tongue, Saul, Saul, why persecutest thou me? it is hard for thee to kick against the pricks.

15 And I said, Who art thou, Lord? And he said, I am Jesus whom thou persecutest.

16 But rise, and stand upon thy feet: for I have appeared unto thee for this purpose, to make thee a minister and a witness both of these things which thou hast seen, and of those things in the which I will appear unto thee;

17 Delivering thee from the people, and from the Gentiles, unto

whom now I send thee,

18 To open their eyes, (and) to turn (them) from darkness to light, and (from) the power of Satan unto God, that they may receive forgiveness of sins, and inheritance among them which are sanctified by faith that is in me.

19 Whereupon, O king Agrippa, I was not disobedient unto the heavenly vision:

REV. 9:17 And thus I saw the horses in the vision, and them that sat on them, having breastplates of fire, and of jacinth, and brimstone: and the heads of the horses (were) as the heads of lions; and out of their mouths issued fire and smoke and brimstone.

Category 7 — Interpretations Come from God

It is God who gives the wisdom and ability to interpret dreams and visions. We are to seek Him for that gift and ability.

GEN 40:5 And they dreamed a dream both of them, each man his dream in one night, each man according to the interpretation of his dream, the butler and the baker of the king of Egypt, which (were) bound in the prison.

6 And Joseph came in unto them in the morning, and looked upon them, and, behold, they (were) sad.

7 And he asked Pharaoh's officers that (were) with him in the ward of his lord's house, saying, Wherefore look ye (so) sadly today?

8 And they said unto him. We have dreamed a dream, and (there is) no interpreter of it. And Joseph said unto them, (Do) not interpretations (belong) to God? tell me (them), I pray you.

9 And the chief butler told his dream to Joseph, and said to him, In my dream, behold, a vine (was) before me;

2 CHRON. 26:5 And he sought God in the days of Zechariah, who had understanding in the visions of God: and as long as he sought the Lord, God made him to prosper.

DAN. 1:17 As for these four children, God gave them knowledge and skill in all learning and wisdom: and Daniel had understanding in all visions and dreams.

DAN. 8:1 In the third year of the reign of king Belshazzar a vision appeared unto me, (even unto) me Daniel, after that which appeared unto me at the first.

2 And I saw in a vision; and it came to pass, when I saw, that I

(was) at Shushan (in) the palace, which (is) in the province of Elam; and I saw in a vision, and I was by the river of Ulai.

3 Then I lifted up mine eyes, and saw, and, behold, there stood before the river a ram which had (two) horns; and the (two) horns (were) high; but one (was) higher than the other, and the higher came up last.

13 Then I heard one saint speaking, and another saint said unto that certain (saint) which spake, How long (shall be) the vision (concerning) the daily (sacrifice), and the transgression of desolation, to give both the sanctuary and the host to be trodden under foot?

15 And it came to pass, when I, (even) I Daniel, had seen the vision, and sought for the meaning, then, behold, there stood before me as the appearance of a man.

16 And I heard a man's voice between (the banks of) Ulai, which called, and said, Gabriel, make this (man) to understand the vision.

17 So he came near where I stood: and when he came, I was afraid, and fell upon my face; but he said unto me, Understand, O son of man: for the time of the end (shall be) the vision.

18 Now as he was speaking with me, I was in a deep sleep on my face toward the ground: but he touched me, and set me upright.

26 And the vision of the evening and the morning which was told (is) true: wherefore shut thou up the vision; for it (shall be) for many days.

27 And I Daniel fainted, and was sick (certain) days; afterward I rose up, and did the king's business; and I was astonished at the vision, but none understood (it).

DAN. 9:21 Yea, while I (was) speaking in prayer, even the man Gabriel, whom I had seen in the vision at the beginning, being caused to fly swiftly, touched me about the time of the evening oblation.

22 And he informed (me), and talked with me, and said, O Daniel, I am not come forth to give thee skill and understanding.

23 At the beginning of thy supplications the commandment came forth, and I am come to shew (thee); for thou (art) greatly beloved: therefore understand the matter, and consider the vision.

24 Seventy weeks are determined upon the people and upon thy holy city, to finish the transgression, and to make an end of sins, and to make reconciliation of iniquity, and to bring in everlasting righteousness, and to seal up the vision and prophecy, and to anoint the most Holy.

DAN. 10:1 In the third year of Cyrus king of Persia a thing was revealed unto Daniel, whose name was called Belteshazzar; and that thing (was) true, but the time appointed (was) long: and he understood the thing, and had understanding of the vision.

5 *Then I lifted up mine eyes,* and looked, and behold a certain man clothed in linen, whose loins (were) girded with fine gold of Uphaz:

6 His body also (was) like the beryl, and his face as the appearance of lightning, and his eyes as lamps of fire, and his arms and his feet like in colour to polished brass, and the voice of his words like the voice of a multitude.

7 *And I Daniel alone saw the vision:* for the men that were with me saw not the vision: but a great quaking fell upon them, so that they fled to hide themselves.

8 Therefore I was left alone, and saw this great vision, and there remained no strength in me: for my comeliness was turned in me into corruption, and I retained no strength.

9 Yet heard I the voice of his words: and when I heard the voice of his words, then I was in a deep sleep on my face, and my face toward the ground.

10 And, behold, a hand touched me, which set me upon my knees and (upon) the palms of my hands.

11 And he said unto me, O Daniel, a man greatly beloved, understand the words that I speak unto thee, and stand upright: for unto thee am I now sent. And when he had spoken this word unto me, I stood trembling.

12 Then said he unto me, Fear not, Daniel: for from the first day that thou didst set thine heart to understand, and to chasten thyself before thy God, thy words were heard, and I am come for thy words.

13 But the prince of the kingdom of Persia withstood me one and twenty days; but, lo, Michael, one of the chief princes came to help me; and I remained there with the kings of Persia.

14 Now I can come to make thee understand what shall befall thy people in the latter days: for yet the vision (is) for (many) days.

15 And when he had spoken such words unto me, I set my face toward the ground, and I became dumb.

16 And, behold, (one) like the similitude of the sons of men touched my lips: then I opened my mouth, and spake, and said unto him that stood before me, O my Lord, by the vision my sorrows are turned upon me, and I have retained no strength.

Category 8 — Testing Dream and Vision

There is a need to test all visions and dreams, and their interpretations, because some men are evil, and because impurities can contaminate our vision.

DEUT 13:1 If there arise among you a prophet, or a dreamer of dreams, and giveth thee a sign or a wonder,

2 And the sign or the wonder come to pass, whereof he spake unto thee, saying, Let us go after other gods, which thou hast not known, and let us serve them:

3 Thou shalt not hearken unto the words of that prophet, or that dreamer of dreams: for the Lord your God proveth you, to know whether ye love the Lord your God with all your heart and with all your soul.

4 Ye shall walk after the Lord your God, and fear him, and keep his commandments, and obey his voice, and ye shall serve him, and cleave unto him.

5 And that prophet, or that dreamer of dreams, shall be put to death; because he hath spoken to turn you away from the Lord your God, which brought you out of the land of Egypt, and redeemed you out of the house of bondage, to thrust thee out of the way which the Lord thy God commanded thee to walk in. So shalt thou put the evil away from the midst of thee.

ISA. 28:7 But they also have erred through wine, and through strong drink are out of the way; the priest and the prophet have erred through strong drink, they are swallowed up of wine, they are out of the way through strong drink; they err in vision, they stumble (in) judgment.

ISA. 30:10 Which say to the seers, See not; and to the prophets, Prophesy not unto us right things, speak unto us smooth things, prophesy deceits:

JER. 14:14 Then the Lord said unto me, The prophets prophesy lies in my name: I sent them not, neither have I commanded them, neither spake unto them: they prophesy unto you a false vision and divination, and a thing of nought, and the deceit of their heart.

JER. 23:16 Thus saith the Lord of hosts, Hearken not unto the words of the prophets that prophesy unto you: they make you vain: they speak a vision of their own heart, (and) not out of the mouth of the Lord.

25 I have heard what the prophets said, that prophesy lies in my name, saying, I have dreamed, I have dreamed.

27 Which think to cause my people to forget my name by their dreams which they tell every man to his neighbour, as their fathers have forgotten my name for Baal.

28 The prophet that hath a dream, let him tell a dream; and he that hath my word, let him speak my word faithfully. What (is) the chaff to the wheat? saith the Lord.

32 Behold, I (am) against them that prophesy false dreams, saith the Lord, and do tell them, and cause my people to err by their lies, and by their lightness; yet I sent them not, nor commanded them: therefore they shall not profit this people at all, saith the Lord.

JER. 27:9 Therefore hearken not ye to your prophets, nor to your diviners, nor to your dreamers, nor to your enchanters, nor to your sorcerers, which speak unto you, saying, Ye shall not serve the king of Babylon:

JER 29:8 For thus saith the Lord of hosts, the God of Israel; Let not your prophets and your diviners, that (be) in the midst of you, deceive you, neither hearken to your dreams which ye cause to be dreamed.
21 Thus saith the Lord of hosts, the God of Israel, of Ahab the son of Kolaiah, and of Zedekiah the son of Maaseiah, which prophesy a lie unto you in my name; Behold, I will deliver them into the hand of Nebuchadnezzar king of Babylon; and he shall slay them before your eyes;

EZEK. 12.2 Son of man, thou dwellest in the midst of a rebellious house, which have eyes to see, and see not; they have ears to hear, and hear not; for they (are) a rebellious house.

EZEK. 12:22 Son of man, what (is) that proverb (that) ye have in the land of Israel, saying, The days are prolonged, and every vision faileth?
23 Tell them therefore, Thus saith the Lord God; I will make this proverb to cease, and they shall no more use it as a proverb in Israel; but say unto them, The days are at hand, and the effect of every vision.
24 For there shall be no more any vain vision nor flattering divination within the house of Israel.
25 For I (am) the Lord; I will speak, and the word that I shall speak shall come to pass; it shall be no more prolonged: for in your days, O rebellious house, will I say the word, and will perform it, saith the Lord God.
26 Again the word of the Lord came to me, saying,
27 Son of man, behold, (they of) the house of Israel say, The vision that he seeth (is) for many days (to come), and he prophesieth of the times (that are) far off.

EZEK. 13:7 Have ye not seen a vain vision, and have ye not spoken a lying divination, whereas ye say, The Lord saith (it); albeit, I have not spoken?
16 (To wit), the prophets of Israel which prophesy concerning

Jerusalem, and which see visions of peace for her, and (there is) no peace, saith the Lord God.

ZECH. 10:2 For the idols have spoken vanity, and the diviners have seen a lie, and have told false dreams; they comfort in vain: therefore they went their way as a flock, they were troubled, because (there was) no shepherd.

Category 9 — The Inner Location of Visionary Experiences

It is very interesting to note in the following verses that man can meet with God and Jesus and angels in visions located in his mind (NASB) or head (KJV), and that these inner encounters are actually considered divine spiritual encounters with heavenly beings.

DAN. 4:5 I saw a dream which made me afraid, and the thoughts upon my bed and the visions of my head troubled me.

6 Therefore made I a decree to bring in all the wise (men) of Babylon before me, that they might make known unto me the interpretation of the dream.

7 Then came in the magicians, the astrologers, the Chaldeans, and the soothsayers: and I told the dream before them; but they did not make known unto me the interpretation thereof.

8 But at the last Daniel came in before me, whose name (was) Belteshazzar, according to the name of my god, and in whom (is) the spirit of the holy gods and before him I told the dream, (saying),

9 O Belteshazzar, master of the magicians, because I know that the spirit of the holy gods (is) in thee, and no secret troubleth thee, tell me the visions of my dream that I have seen, and the interpretation thereof.

10 Thus (were) the visions of mine head in my bed; I saw, and behold a tree in the midst of the earth, and the height thereof (was) great.

13 I saw in the *visions of my head* upon my bed, and, behold, a watcher and a holy one came down from heaven.

18 This dream I king Nebuchadnezzar have seen. Now thou, O Belteshazzar, declare the interpretation thereof, forasmuch as all the wise (men) of my kingdom are not able to make known unto me the interpretation: but thou (art) able; for the spirit of the holy gods (is) in thee.

19 Then Daniel, whose name (was) Belteshazzar, was astonied for one hour, and his thoughts troubled him. The king spake, and said, Belteshazzar, let not the dream, or the interpretation thereof, trouble

thee. Belteshazzar answered and said, My lord, the dream (be) to them that hate thee, and the interpretation thereof to thine enemies.

DAN. 5:12 Forasmuch as an excellent spirit, and knowledge, and understanding, interpreting of dreams, and shewing of hard sentences, and dissolving of doubts, were found in the same Daniel, whom the king named Belteshazzar; now let Daniel be called, and he will shew the interpretation.

DAN. 7:1 In the first year of Belshazzar king of Babylon Daniel had a dream, (and) told the sum of the matters.

2 Daniel spake and said, I saw in my vision by night, and, behold, the four winds of the heaven strove upon the great sea.

7 After this I saw in the night visions, and behold a fourth beast, dreadful and terrible, and strong exceedingly; and it had great iron teeth: it devoured and brake in pieces, and stamped the residue with the feet of it; and it (was) diverse from all the beasts that (were) before it; and it had ten horns.

13 I saw in the night visions, and, behold, (one) like the Son of man came with the clouds of heaven, and came to the Ancient of days, and they brought him near before him.

15 I Daniel was grieved in my spirit in the midst of (my) body, and the visions of my head troubled me.

MY PERSONAL REFLECTIONS ON DREAM AND VISION

by Mark Virkler

As I have already written extensively on developing dream and vision in **Biblical Research Concerning Dreams and Visions; Communion with God; Communion with God Study Guide; Dialoguing with God; Pure in Heart; Abiding in Christ; Developing Heart Faith; and A Philosophy of Christian Education** I will not seek to repeat all my earlier conclusions, but I will seek to add some new reflections.

1. God does speak to us through dream and vision, as attested by hundreds of verses.

2. Jesus lived in a **constant** flow of divine images, as He "only did that which He **saw** the Father doing (Jn. 5:19,20)."

3. Since Jesus is our perfect example, we are to learn to live the way He did, that is, constantly open to the divine flow of vision.

4. The Bible tells us that God provides a ready and free flow of dreams and visions, as we experience the outpouring of the Holy Spirit. Therefore, the **normal Christian life is to experience vision readily** (Acts 2:17).

5. Samuel established schools of the prophets, to train men to become seers (the original term for prophets). There is no indication that this process would not be continued. Today there are many Schools of the Prophets, once again training men and women to become seers.

6. The best way to train a person to become a seer is to train him to become a "looker." You will find scores of references from both Old and New Testament prophets saying "I looked." Probably the major reason people are not seers today is because no one is instructing them to become lookers. We must once again learn to look to see....

7. We are commanded especially to fix our eyes upon Jesus (Heb. 12:1,2). That surely could include a literal focusing of the eyes of our heart upon Him in a visionary way.

8. It is proper to prime the pump as we look for vision, as evidenced by:

    a. John's account in Revelation 4:1 - "I looked." He then found himself in the Spirit in Rev. 4:2 with a divine flow of vision taking over.

    b. The prophets' constant statement "I looked."

    c. The fact that we have not if we ask not. The looking itself is the act that often opens us up to seeing.

9. God uses images extensively in His communion with us, as evidenced by:

a.   The fact that the Bible is a picture book (that is, a collection of true stories about people's lives), and not primarily a book of systematic theology. We are able to enter each story and allow God the opportunity to speak to us from the midst of the story. A story is a flow of images woven together. Therefore, when God wrote His revelation to man, He chose images over analytical thought as a primary mode of communication.

b.   Jesus Himself was an image (Col. 1:15). He "was the image of the invisible God." Therefore, when God sought to most clearly communicate Himself to man, He chose the form of an image.

c.   When God designed the holy of holies, the place where man would stand directly before the presence of God, God used an **image** to represent Himself to Moses and the other high priests. If God were opposed to the use of images to represent Himself to man He could have had Moses stand alone in an empty room and speak to him face to face and mouth to mouth without the use of images. However, God chose to use an image, the ark of the covenant and the mercy seat with cherubim on top. Therefore, God Himself has chosen to use images when communicating Himself to man, not only in the ark of the covenant in the Old Testament but now in His son Jesus, the image of the invisible God. Therefore I believe that the proper image for the New Testament believer, as he comes and stands before God, is Jesus of Nazareth, or one of John's visions of the glorified Jesus, as found in the book of Revelation.

d.   God's use of types throughout the Old Testament.

e.   Jesus' constant use of parables (picture stories) as He taught (Matt. 13:34).

10. I believe it is proper to enter into the image or picture to meet God in a direct spiritual encounter because:

a.   John did it as he primed the pump in Rev. 4:1, resulting in the flow of divine images taking over, an experience which he called "being in Spirit."

b.   The structure of the entire Bible is such as to lead one into this experience. As we have noted earlier the Bible is primarily a picture book, rather than a book of analytical theology. We are commanded to come unto the Lord as little children. When a child reads a story he pictures the entire thing as he reads it. Most adults do so as well. According to Eph.

1:18,19, God desires to open the eyes of our hearts, granting us a spirit of wisdom and of revelation as we study. God desires to speak into our hearts as we study His word. Therefore I see the entire process of Bible Study, as God has designed it, to involve visualization, and God speaking to us out of the midst of the image (created by the Word) which is set before our eyes.

11. I believe that as the vision within our hearts comes alive, the divine flow represents an actual encounter between us and God, Christ and His angels.

    a.   In Dan. 4:13,14 we find King Nebuchadnezzar encountering an angel in a vision **in his mind.** "I was looking in the visions **in my mind** as I lay on my bed, and behold, an angelic watcher, a holy one, descended from heaven. He shouted out and spoke as follows...."

    b.   In Dan. 7:1, 13 and 15 we find that Daniel encountered the Ancient of Days and one like a Son of Man in a vision he had **in his mind.** "In the first year of Belshazzar king of Babylon Daniel saw a dream and visions **in his mind** as he lay on his bed; then he wrote the dream down and related the flowing summary of it . . . I kept looking in the night visions, and behold, with the clouds of heaven one like a Son of Man was coming, and he came up to the Ancient of Days and was presented before Him . . . As for me, Daniel, my spirit was distressed within me, and the visions **in my mind** kept alarming me."

    c.   Therefore I believe as we are led to encounter God, Christ and angels in the visions of our minds as we meditate on the Word of God, these visions can and do come alive and constitute an actual encounter between God and man.

12. I believe our ability to see in the Spirit was designed to be presented to God and filled by God.

    a.   We know that everything that God created was good, and that **everything** obviously has to include our visionary capacity. As all that God has created is presented before Him to fill, God's kingdom is realized and His purposes established. As we present the eyes of our hearts to Him to fill, His vision fills our hearts. Our responsibility is to present all our capacities quietly before Him, allowing Him to move upon and through them. That includes our minds, our hearts, our hands, our mouths, and our visionary capacity, along with everything else that we are.

    b.   God generally will not force Himself upon the one who is not opening himself before Him. We generally will not speak in tongues until we offer Him our mouths. We generally will not receive words of wisdom and knowledge until we offer Him our minds. We generally will not receive visions until we offer Him the eyes of our hearts.

c.   **Therefore, in cultivating our visionary capacity, we are presenting the eyes of our hearts before God, asking Him to fill them.**

13.   In the Greek New Testament there were many Greek words and phrases used to describe encountering God through dream and vision and experiencing revelation. They are:

a.   "Onar" - a common word for "dream." Precisely, it is a vision seen in sleep as opposed to waking. Used in Matt. 1:20; 2:12,13,19,22; 27:19.

b.   "Enupnion" - a vision seen in sleep. It stresses the giveness, almost surprise quality, of what is received in sleep. Used in Acts 2:17 and Jude 8.

c.   "Horama" - translated vision. It can refer to visions of the night or sleeping experiences, as well as to waking visions. Used in Matthew 17:9; Acts 7:31; 9:10,12; 10:3,17,19; 11:5; 12:9; 16:9, 10; 18:9.

d.   "Opasis" - can signify the eye as the organ of sight, an appearance of any kind, even a spectacle, but there are also two instances where it means a supernatural vision (Acts 2:17 and Revelation 9:17). The distinction between the perception of the physical and the nonphysical is lacking in the Greek. Both "seeings" are genuine perception.

e.   "Optasia" - translated vision. It has the sense of self-disclosure, of "letting oneself be seen." It is used in the following four passages, Luke 1:22; 24:23; Acts 26:19; II Corinthians 12:1.

f.   "Ekstasis" - is the word from which the English word "ecstasy" is derived. It means literally standing aside from oneself, being displaced or over against oneself, and ordinarily there is a sense of amazement, confusion, and even of extreme terror. It may refer to either sleeping or waking experiences, and psychologically both the dreams of sleep and the imagery that occurs on the border of wakefulness, hypnagogic or hypnopompic imagery, fit the condition that "ekstasis" describes. Although translated "trance" it is misleading to use the word "trance" as a direct translation. It is used in Mark 5:42; Luke 5:26; Mark 16:8; Acts 3:10; 10:10; 11:5; 22:17.

g.   "Ginomai en pneumati" - translated "to become in Spirit" (Rev. 1:10). This signified a state in which one could see visions and be informed or spoken to directly by the Spirit. Related phrases are found in Matt. 4:1; Mark 1:12; Luke 4:1 and Luke 1:41.

h.   "Ephistemi, Paristemi" - simply referring to the fact that some reality stands by in the night or in the day. Used in Acts 23:11; 27:23; Luke 1:11; Acts 10:30; 16:9.

i.   "Angelos" - or angel, literally meaning an actual physical envoy, a messenger, or a divine being sent by God, and "daimon, daimonion, diabolos" or demon, devil, and Satan, literally refer to non-physical entities or powers from satan. Both angels and satan can be encountered in dreams and visionary experiences as shown in the following references: Acts 10:3; Jude 8; and many instances in the book of Revelation.

j.   "Blepo" and "eido" mean "to see," "to perceive." These words are used to mean "see" in the normal outer sense, yet are also used to refer to seeing in the spiritual sense as evidenced in the following passages: Rev. 1:2,11; Mark 9:9; Luke 9:36. Obviously, because of the dual use of these words to describe both inner and outer sight, the early church considered visionary experiences just as easy to see and observe, and just as much given and as valid, as the perceptions one has of the outer physical world.

k.   "Apokalupsis" - translated "revelation" literally means disclosure, divine uncovering, or revelation. It is used in Romans 16:25; I Cor. 14:6,26; II Cor. 12:1,7 and Gal. 2:2.

When considering the great variety of words used by New Testament Christians to describe their visionary experiences we see that they have a vast number to select from, allowing them to very precisely define the exact type of visionary encounter they were having. Probably **our** poverty of vocabulary to even find one or two suitable words to clearly define our inner, visionary experience, demonstrates the poverty of direct spiritual encounter we all experience in the Western culture.

May we restore to our vocabulary and to our experience a host of suitable words to clearly define the variety of inner spiritual experiences we are having.

DREAMS AND VISIONS THROUGHOUT CHURCH HISTORY

By Mark Virkler

In order to give you a clearer view of the church's experience with dreams and visions throughout the last 2000 years I offer the following examples.

1. **Augustine** Rather than ignoring dreams as the contemporary church has done, Augustine took the entire Twelfth book in his **De Genesi ad Litteram** to explain his understanding of dreams and visions.

2. **Polycarp** The book **Martyrdom of Polycarp** tells of Polycarp praying not long before his martyrdom, and being informed of what was shortly to happen through a symbolic vision. He saw the pillow under his head catch fire and realized that this image of destruction signified his own impending capture and death.

3. **Justin Martyr** In his writings Martyr says that dreams are sent by spirits. He believed that dreams are sent by both evil spirits and God.

4. **Irenaeus** As Irenaeus refuted gnostic speculation in his writings, he indicated his clear view concerning dreams and the life of the Christian. In his principal work, **Against Heresies,** Irenaeus commented appreciatively and intelligently on the dream of Peter in Acts 10; he believed that the dream itself was a proof of the authenticity of Peter's experience. Again, he stressed the authenticity of Paul's dream at Troas. He also inferred from the dreams of Joseph in Matthew that Joseph's dreaming showed how close he was to the real God. In still another place he explained that although God is Himself invisible to the eye directly, he gives us visions and dreams through which he conveys the likeness of His nature and His glory.

5. **Clement** In discussing the nature and meaning of sleep, Clement urged: "Let us not, then, who are sons of the true light, close the door against this light; but turning in on ourselves, illumining the eyes of the hidden man, and gazing on the truth itself, and receiving its streams, let us clearly and intelligibly reveal such dreams as are true....Thus also such dreams as are true, in the view of him who reflects rightly, are the thoughts of a sober soul, undistracted for the time by the affections of the body, and counselling with itself in the best manner....Wherefore always contemplating God, and by perpetual converse with Him innoculating the body with wakefulness, it raises man to equality with angelic grace, and from the practice of wakefulness it grasps the eternity of life" (Taken from the **Stromata, or Miscellanies**).

6. **Origen** In his great answer to the pagans, **Against Celsus,** Origen defended the visions of the Bible, saying: "....We, nevertheless, so far as we can, shall support our position, maintaining that, as it is a matter of belief that in a dream impressions have been brought before the minds of many, some relating to divine things, and others to future events of this life, and this either with clearness or in an enigmatic manner, a fact which is manifest to all who accept the doctrine of providence: so how is it absurd to say that the mind which could receive impressions in a dream should be impressed also in a waking vision, for the benefit either of him on whom the impressions are made, or of those who are to hear the account of them from him?" Having satisfied his parallel between dreams and visions, Origen then went on to discuss the nature of dreams.

In His **Contra Celsus** Origen declared that many Christians had been converted from their pagan ways by this kind of direct break-through into their lives in waking visions and dreams of the night. He made it clear that many such instances were known of this sort of conversion.

7. **Tertullian** Tertullian devoted eight chapters of his work **A Treatise on the Soul,** or **De anima** to his study of sleep and dreams. He believed that all dream and evidenced it by the movement of sleeping infants. He believed that dreams occur from four sources: demons, God, natural dreams that the soul creates, and finally "the ecstatic state and its peculiar conditions" or in other words, the unconscious. Furthermore he states, "And thus we - who both acknowledge and reverence, even as we do the prophecies, modern visions as equally promised to us, and consider the other powers of the Holy Spirit as an agency of the Church for which also He was sent, administering all gifts in all, even as the Lord distributed to every one...."

8. **Thascius Cyprian** Bishop of Carthage in 250 A.D. In a letter he wrote to Florentius Pupianus he said, "Although I know that to some men dreams seem ridiculous and visions foolish, yet assuredly it is to such as would rather believe in opposition to the priest, than believe the priest." In another letter he wrote that God guides the very councils of the church by "many and manifest visions." He commended the reader Celerinus because his conversion to the church had come through a vision of the night.

9. **Lactantius** Chosen by Constantine the Great to tutor his son. In his **Divine Institutes** he included a chapter on "The Use of Reason in Religion; and of Dreams, Auguries, Oracles, and Similar Portents," in which he cited examples to show that through dreams a knowledge of the future is occasionally given to pagans as well as to Christians. His example of a logical fallacy is that of a man who has dreamed that he ought not believe in dreams.

10. **Constantine** Lactantius writes of the heavenly vision that gave Constantine his great victory in 300 A.D. The story begins with Constantine being in desperate need and calling on God for help. "Accordingly he called on Him with earnest prayer and supplications that he would reveal to him Who He was, and stretch forth His right hand to help him in his present difficulties. And while he was thus praying with fervent entreaty, a most marvelous sign appeared to him from heaven, the account of which it might have been hard to believe had it been related by any other person. But since the victorious emperor himself long afterwards declared it to the writer of this history, when he was honored with his acquaintance and society, and confirmed his statement by an oath, who could hesitate to accredit the relation especially since the testimony of after-time has established its truth? He said that about noon, when the day was already beginning to decline, he saw with his own eyes the trophy of a cross of light in the heavens, above the sun, and bearing the inscription, CONQUER BY THIS. At this sight he himself was struck with amazement, and his whole army also, which followed him on this expedition, and witnessed the miracle.

He said, moreover, that he doubted within himself what the import of this apparition could be. And while he continued to ponder the reason on its meaning, night suddenly came on; then in his sleep the Christ of God appeared to him with the same sign which he had seen in the heavens, and commanded him to make a likeness of that sign which he had seen in the heavens, and to use it as a safeguard in all engagements with his enemies.

At dawn of day he arose, and communicated the marvel to his friends: and then, calling together the workers in gold and precious stones, he sat in the midst of them, and described to them the figure of the sign he had seen, bidding them represent it in gold and precious stones. And this representation I myself have had an opportunity of seeing." Taken from **The Life of Constantine I, 28-30.**

11. **Socrates** One of the dreams that Socrates mentioned was one by Ignatius of Antioch. Ignatius had had a vision of angels who sang hymns in alternate chants, and so introduced the mode of antiphonal singing. Taken from **Ecclesiastical History Volume 35 and 6**, by Theodoret.

12. **Athanasius** Bishop of Alexandria from 328 to 373. In his great masterpiece of Christian apology, **Against the Heathen,** he wrote: "Often when the body is quiet, and at rest and asleep, man moves inwardly, and beholds what is outside himself, travelling to other countries, walking about, meeting his acquaintances, and often by these means divining and forecasting the actions of the day. But to what can this be due save to the rational soul, in which man thinks of and perceives things beyond himself? . . .

For if even when united and coupled with the body it is not shut in or commensurate with the small dimensions of the body, but often, when the body lies in bed, not moving, but in death-like sleep, the soul keeps awake by virtue of its own power, and transcends the natural power of the body, and as though travelling away from the body while remaining in it, imagines and beholds things above the earth, and often even holds converse with the saints and angels who are above earthly and bodily existence, and approaches them in the confidence of the purity of its intelligence; shall it not all the more, when separated from the body at the time appointed by God Who coupled them together, have its knowledge of immortality more clear?" II.31.5 and 33.3

13. **Gregory of Nyssa** In his major philosphical work, **On the Making of Man,** Gregory deals directly with the meaning and place of sleep and dreams in man's life. He believed that when man is asleep, the senses and the reason rest and the less rational parts of the soul appear to take over. Reason is not, however, extinguished, but smoulders like a fire "heaped with chaff," and then breaks forth with insights that modern dream research calls "secondary mentation." He went on to say that "while all men are guided by their own minds, there are some few who are deemed worthy of evident Divine communication; so, while the imagination of sleep naturally occurs in a like and equivalent manner for all, some, not all, share by means of their dreams in some more Divine manifestation . . ." His reasoning was that there is a natural foreknowledge that comes in an unknown way through the non-rational part of the soul - the "unconscious," according to modern depth psychology - and it is through this part of the soul that God communicates Himself directly.

Gregory then enumerated the other meanings that dreams can have, offering quite a complete outline of the subject. He suggested that dreams can provide mere reminiscences of daily occupations and events. Or, they can reflect the condition of the body, its hunger or thirst, or the emotional condition of the personality. Dreams can also be understood in medical practice as giving clues to the sickness of the body. Indeed, far from stating a superstitious belief, Gregory laid out quite well the principle upon which today's analytical study of dreams is based.

Gregory also told, in a sermon entitled "In Praise of the Forty Martyrs," of a dream that occurred while he was attending a celebration in honor of the soldiers who had been martyred. In the dream the martyrs challenged Gregory for his Christian lethargy and it had a profound effect upon his life.

It is clear that philosophically, practically, and personally Gregory of Nyssa believed the dream could be a revelation of depths beyond the human ego.

14. **Basil the Great** In his commentary on Isaiah, Basil states, "The

enigmas in dreams have a close affinity to those things which are signified in an allegoric or hidden sense in the Scriptures. Thus both Joseph and Daniel, through the gift of prophecy, used to interpret dreams, since the force of reason by itself is not powerful enough for getting at truth." (S. Basili Magni, **Commentarium in Isaiam Prophetam,** Prooemium 6f., J.-P. Migne, Patrologiae Graecae, Paris, 1880, Vol. 30, Col. 127-30).

That Basil believed in continuing to consider dreams is indicated by the letter he wrote to a woman in which he interpreted the dream she had sent him. He suggested to her that her dream meant she was to spend more time in "spiritual contemplation and cultivating that mental vision by which God is won't to be seen."

15. **Gregory of Nazianzen** In his second book of poems Gregory writes "And God summoned me from boyhood in my nocturnal dreams, and I arrived at the very goals of wisdom" (S. Gregorii Theologi, **Carminum,** Liber II, 994-950). In another place he told that this nocturnal vision was the hidden spark that set his whole life aflame for God. In one of his poems he spoke of the ability of demons to also speak through one's dreams. "Devote not your trust too much to the mockery of dreams, Nor let yourself be terrified by everything; Do not become inflated by joyful visions, For frequently a demon prepares these snares for you." (**Carminum,** Liber I, 608-9, lines 209-12).

16. **St. John Chrysostom** In his commentary on Acts volume one he states, "To some the grace was imparted through dreams, to others it was openly poured forth. For indeed by dreams the prophets saw, and received revelations." According to Chrysostom dreams are sent to those whose wills are compliant to God, for they do not need visions or the more startling divine manifestations, and he mentioned Joseph, the father of Jesus, and Peter and Paul as examples of this truth (**Homilies on Matthew,** IV.10f., 18; v.5).

17. **Synesius of Cyrene** Synesius wrote an entire book on dreams. He said, "One man learns . . . while awake, another while asleep. But in the waking state man is the teacher, whereas it is God who makes the dreamer fruitful with His own courage, so that learning and attaining are one and the same. Now to make fruitful is even more than to teach." (Augustine Fitzgerald, **The Essays and Hymns of Synesius of Cyrene,** London, Oxford University Press, 1930, p. 332 [from **Concerning Dreams**]).

Synesius laid out a sound reason for discussing dreams, and then enumerated the blessings to be gained from studying them. For the pure soul who receives impressions clearly, a proper study of dreams gives knowledge of the future with all that this implies. Important information is also provided about bodily malfunction and how it can be corrected. Far more important, this undertaking brings the soul to consider immaterial things, and so, even though it was begun merely to provide knowledge of the future, it turns the soul to God and develops a love of Him. Synesius also told how dreams had helped him in his writings and in his other endeavors, and how they often gave hope to men who had been oppressed by the difficulties of life.

He made fun of people who relied on the popular dream books, insisting that only by constantly checking dreams with experience could they be understood. Their essential nature is personal, and they must be understood by the dreamer in terms of his own life. Some of them seem to be direct revelations of God, but there are also many dreams that are obscure and difficult to interpret. He suggested that anyone who is serious in studying them should keep a record so that he knows his sleeping life as well as his waking one. He even saw the connection between mythology and dreams and explained his belief that the myth is based upon the dream; a true interest in mythology helps a man find the more vital meaning in his own dreams. Finally, Synesius showed the reason for his belief that dreams give hints about eternal life. As the sleeping state is to the waking one, so the life of the soul after death is to the dream life, and thus this state gives some idea of the kind of life that is led by the soul after death.

18. **Ambrose** In Ambrose's famous letter to Theodosius calling for his repentance, he declared that God in a dream forbade him to celebrate communion before the Emperor unless he repented. These are his dramatic words: "I am writing with my own hand that which you alone may read . . . I have been warned, not by man, nor through man, but plainly by Himself that this is forbidden me. For when I was anxious, in the very night in which I was preparing to set out, you appeared to me in a dream to have come into the Church, and I was not permitted to offer the sacrifice . . . Our God gives warnings in many ways, by heavenly signs, by the precepts of the prophets, by the visions even of sinners he wills that we should understand, that we should entreat Him to take away all disturbances . . . that the faith and peace of the Church . . . may continue" (St. Ambrose, Letter LI, 14).

Augustine tells how God revealed to St. Ambrose in a dream the hidden location of two martyred saints, who were then retrieved and given a proper consecration (St. Ambrose, Letter XXII; St. Augustine, **The Confessions,** IX [VII] 16; **The City of God,** XXII.8).

In St. Ambrose's more theological writings Ambrose showed that an angel who speaks through a dream is functioning at the direction of the Holy Spirit, since angelic powers are subject to and moved by the Spirit.

19. **Augustine** As has already been mentioned in number 1 of this series, Augustine wrote widely concerning the place and understanding of dreams in the Christian's life. His study of perception was as sophisticated as any in the ancient world. He saw reality as consisting of outer physical

objects to which we react with our bodies, and then of the impressions of this sense experience, impressions that are "mental" in nature. We then have the inner perception of this sense experience, and finally the mental species in its remembered form. It is the action of the ego that unites these perceptions to the object. In one place he calls the faculty of imagination the bridge that mediates the object to consciousness, thus presenting almost the same thinking as that worked out by Synesius of Cyrene. Augustine saw man as possessing an outward eye that receives and mediates sense impressions, and an inward eye that observes and deals with these collected and stored "mental" realities that are called memory.

In addition to the realities that come from outer perception and from inner perception of "memories," autonomous spiritual realities (angels and demons) can present themselves directly to the inner eye. These are of the same nature as the stored "mental" or psychic realities that are perceived inwardly. Augustine writes that men in sleep or trance can experience contents that come from memory "or some other hidden force through certain spiritual commixtures of a similarly spiritual substance" (St. Augustine, **On the Trinity,** XI.4.7). These autonomous realities are non-physical; yet they can either assume a corporeal appearance and be experienced through the outward eye, or be presented directly to consciousness through the inner eye in dreams, visions, and trances. Thus through dreams man is presented with a whole storehouse of unconscious memories and spontaneous contents; he is given access to a world that the fathers called the realm of the spirit.

Just as angels have direct contact with man's psyche and present their messages before the inner eye, so also do demons. "They persuade [men], however, in marvelous and unseen ways, entering by means of that subtlety of their own bodies into the bodies of men who are unaware, and through certain imaginary visions mingling themselves with men's thoughts whether they are awake or asleep (**The Divination of Demons,** V.9, N.Y., Fathers of the Church, Inc., 1955, Vol. 27, p. 430).

In addition to presenting a theory of dreams and visions, Augustine also discussed many examples of providential dreams in the course of his writings. One of the most important of them was the famous dream of his mother Monica, in which she saw herself standing on a measuring device while a young man whose face shone with a smile approached her. She was crying, and when he asked why, she told of her sorrow that her son turned away from Christ. He told her to look, and suddenly she saw Augustine standing on the same rule with her and she was comforted. Realizing the significance of the symbolism, she was able to go on praying for him with patience and hope; her dreams and visions are also mentioned in several other places in **The Confessions** (**The Confessions,** III.19, V.17, VI.23, VIII.30).

20. **Jerome** In his early life Jerome was torn between reading the classics and the Bible until he had this dream. "Suddenly I was caught up in the spirit and dragged before the judgment seat of the Judge; and here the light was so bright, and those who stood around were so radiant, that I cast myself upon the ground and did not dare to look up. Asked who and what I was I replied: 'I am a Christian.' But he who presided said: "Thou liest, thou art a follower of Cicero and not of Christ. For 'where thy treasure is, there will thy heart be also.' Instantly I became dumb, and amid the strokes of the lash-for He had ordered me to be scourged - I was tortured more severely still by the fire of conscience, considering with myself that verse, 'In the grave who shall give thee thanks?' Yet for all that I began to cry and to bewail myself, saying: 'Have mercy upon me, O Lord: have mercy upon me.' Amid the sound of the scourges this cry still made itself heard. At last the bystanders, falling down before the knees of Him who presided, prayed that He would have pity on my youth, and that he would give me space to repent of my error. He might still, they urged, inflict torture on me, should I ever again read the works of the Gentiles . . .

Accordingly I made an oath and called upon His name, saying: 'Lord, if ever again I possess worldly books, or if ever again I read such, I have denied Thee.' Dismissed, then, on taking this oath, I returned to the upper world, and to the surprise of all, I opened upon them eyes so drenched world, and to the surprise of all, I opened upon them eyes so drenched with tears that my distress served to convince even the incredulous. And that this was no sleep nor idle dream, such as those by which we are often mocked, I call to witness the tribunal before which I lay, and the terrible judgment which I feared...I profess that my shoulders were black and blue, that I felt the bruises long after I awoke from my sleep, and that thenceforth I read the books of God with a zeal greater than I had previously given to the books of men (St. Jerome, Letter XXII, To Ekustochium, 30).

Jerome's studies also gave him good reason to value dreams and visions. In commenting on Jeremiah 23:25ff., he shared Jeremiah's concern, indicating that dreaming is a kind of prophesying that God can use as one vehicle of revelation to a soul. It can be a valuable revelation from God if a man's life is turned toward him. But dreams can become idolatrous when they are sought and interpreted for their own sake by one who is serving his own self-interest instead of God. The value of the dream depends upon the person who seeks it and the person who interprets it. Sometimes God sends dreams to the unrighteous, like those of Nebuchadnezzar and Pharaoh, so that the servants of God may manifest their wisdom. Thus it is the duty of those who have the word of the Lord to explain dreams (S. Eusebii Hieronymi, **Commentariorum in Jeremiam Prophetam**, IV.23).

This word could not be sought, however, by pagan practices. In commenting on Isaiah 65:4, Jerome went along with the prophet and condemned people who "sit in the graves and the temples of idols where they are accustomed to stretch out on the skins of sacrificial animals in order to know the future by dreams, abominations which are still practiced today in the temples of Aescylapius (**Commentariorum in Isaiam Prophetam**). Later, however, in the discussion of Galatians, he brought up specifically the dream in Acts 16 in which Paul "was given the true light (lucam vero)." (**Commentariorum in Epistolam ad Galatos, 1**).

Jerome made no distinction at all between the vision and the dream. Yet in the end he fixed the ground firmly that would justify a growing fear of these experiences. In translating Leviticus 19:26 and Deuteronomy 18:10 with one word different from other passages, a direct mistranslation, (the word [anan] occurs ten times in the Old Testament. In most cases in the current versions it is simply translated "soothsayer or soothsaying,") Jerome turned the law: "You shall not practice augury or witchcraft (i.e., soothsaying)" into the prohibition: "You shall not practice augury nor observe dreams." Thus by the authority of the Vulgate, dreams were classed with soothsaying, the practice of listening to them with other superstitious ideas.

From here we enter the 1000 year period known as the Dark Ages, and little more is said until the writings of Thomas Aquinas.

21. Thomas Aquinas Aquinas was greatly influenced by Aristotle, and sought to reduce Christianity into Aristotle's world view. This world view left no room for direct spiritual encounter. Therefore dreams and visions were played down, along with experiences of angels and demons, the healings, tongue speaking, and miracles. In the end Aquinas' life contradicted what he had written. He did come into direct relationship with God, and ceased to write and dictate. When he was urged to go on, he replied: "I can do no more; such things have been revealed to me that all I have written seems as straw, and I now await the end of my life" (**Great Books of the Western World,** Vol. 19[Thomas Aquinas], Chicago, Encyclopedia Britannica, Inc., 1952, p.vi).

This was the turning point for the church concerning its view of dreams and their ability to carry forth revelation from Almighty God into the believer's life. Although the church has flip-flopped back and forth somewhat concerning its view on the value of dreams, the pervading view today is much in line with the rationalism of our day, and very much out of line with the teachings of Scripture, and the early church fathers. So much so that one actually appears strange to believe that God would actually communicate today to His children through the medium of dreams and visions. I will close this section with just a couple more modern day accounts of dreams and revelation.

22. Abraham Lincoln Abraham Lincoln dreamed just days before his assasination concerning his impending death.

There are many more modern examples which could be quoted but that is not the purpose at this time. There are entire books on the market today concerning both a Christian's philosophical and theological base for interpreting dreams, as well as testimonial books concerning the variety of dreams and visions being experienced in the Church today.

As we have seen over and over again dreams and visions are considered interchangeable, and so even though much of this research deals primarily with dreams it should be viewed in a wider scope so as to include visions also.

It is time for the Church to return to a biblical understanding of dreams and visions and revelation.

STICKY QUESTIONS

By Mark Virkler

In consideration of the concepts of vision and visualization, there are difficult questions which need to be addressed. What is the difference between divinely birthed vision, and visualization? What about creating through use of a visualized goal held before your mind? Is visualization cultish, evil, demonic? Or is visualization Godly, and Divine?

Webster defines visualization as the "formation of mental visual images, the act or process of interpreting in visual terms or of putting into visible form (**Webster's Ninth New Collegiate Dictionary**). Many Westerners are just beginning to identify the fact that they can think in terms of pictures as well as in terms of analytical rational thought. We have always been able to think both ways; however, only recently have a greater percentage of those in the Western culture begun to define and identify this process of thinking with pictures. As it is being reintroduced into the Church, we need to examine the process, and discern how God wants to use our visionary capacity.

Our God-given ability to sing is neither good nor evil in itself. Such classification is dependent upon the one to whom this ability is yielded. If it is yielded to satan, he will use it to produce evil; if it is yielded to God, He will use it to produce good. If it is not consciously yielded to either God or satan, it will be a manifestation of the self. However, I am convinced that what is not yielded to God will eventually be confiscated by satan.

It seems to me that both the ability to think analytically and the capacity to be visionary are abilities which God has created and placed within man. Neither is evil. Both were created by God and designed to be filled by Him. When God had finished His creation, He said it was **good**. Therefore, the visionary and analytical abilities within mankind are **both** good, when used properly.

The biblical way for man to function is to yield himself to the flow of God through him. That was the whole intent of the Garden of Eden, that man would live in close fellowship with Almighty God. However, man chose to live out of himself, and thus violated his function in life.

Now man **thinks** on his own. He **visions** on his own. He counsels out of his own wisdom, he rules his own life. However, his wisdom is not perfect, his vision is not clear, his counsel is not sure. In separating himself from God, he has lost the creative flow of the Divine life within.. Now he flows out of himself. And the flow is very limited. Not that there is no creative flow. No, God has created man with a spirit, and out of that spirit man can create on a limited scale those things man wants. However, he no longer is flowing with the fullness of creativity that God intended.

Yes, man can go to school for 12 or 16 or 18 years, and acquire much knowledge and wisdom, but it may not be **God's** wisdom. Yes, man can build his own vision and experience the flow of creative ability, but it may not be the fullness of **God's** vision and creativity. Yes, man can reason theologically with his own mind, but he may not find the truth, which is **of God**. Yes, man can dream a dream of his own choosing, but it may not be **God's** dream.

The question is not analytical thought over visionary thought, but rather, man choosing to do his own thinking and visioning, rather than letting our Heavenly Father flow through his reasoning capacity with words of wisdom and words of knowledge, and letting God flow through his visionary capacity with dream and vision.

God desires man to yield both his reasoning and visionary capacities to Him to fill. That was the design. That was the intention.

But now we begin to run into some problems. How far can we deviate from God's original design and avoid reaping the destruction that comes from going our own way? Can man reason on his own? Can man envision on his own? I'm not sure that this is God's choicest desire. However, I am sure that we, as the Church, can squabble about it for a good many years to come, if we allow ourselves to. I believe God's preference is that we put forth a Divine call for each child of God to present his natural reasoning and visionary abilities to God, to allow Him to flow through them, by the working of the Holy Spirit.

Let us not reason outside of the presence of the Holy Spirit, for this only results in death (Ps. 73:1-16). Let us, instead, come into the sanctuary of Almighty God and begin **perceiving** His revelation in our hearts and minds (Ps. 73:17). May we learn to let the flow of the Spirit guide our thoughts, so that the mind of Christ is released through our lives.

Let us not envision outside of the presence of Almighty God. Let us come to Him and let Him form the vision within our hearts. Then the Kingdom of God can be released through our lives.

We have another problem within the Church. **Many in the church have trouble hearing the voice of God and seeing the vision of the Almighty.** The solution, I believe, has been evolving over this last century.

In the early 1900's the Pentecostal movement was born, the discovery was made afresh that dreams, visions and revelation are indeed **for today.** Many in the Church received this as a theological point of view but had no idea how to appropriate it experientially in their own lives, thus allowing dream, vision, and prophecy to flow normally, easily, and freely through their hearts.

In recent years pioneers have begun to find creative ways to teach the Church how to become open to the experience of visions and revelations through their hearts. Some say these men have drawn from Jung, who himself drew from occult sources. Personally, I do not care how many cult or occult sources happen to believe a truth I carry. I don't even care if satan himself believes it. All I care about is whether the Bible teaches it, or

FOUR POSITIONS WE CAN TAKE
AS WE WALK THROUGH LIFE
WHICH POSITION IS YOURS?

RATIONALISM

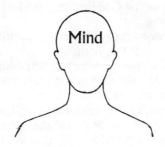

Rational thinking is idolized and visionary or mystical encounter is scorned.

MYSTICISM

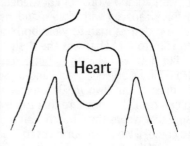

Visionary and mystical encounter are idolized and rational thought is scorned.

HUMANISM

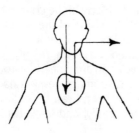

Rational thought and visualization are both used to further one's own ends and goals.

CHRISTIANITY

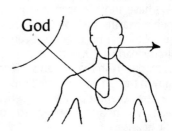

Rational and visionary capacities are both yielded to God to fill and flow through his life.

at least allows for it. The Bible says that even the demons believe that there is one God, yet they tremble. (James 2:19). If I am going to throw out every belief that a demon believes I will have nothing left to believe. It is a pointless argument to count how many cults believe a particular truth of Christianity.

Let us come back to examining the Word, and see if the Bible either teaches or allows the belief in that which is being questioned. Obviously, the Bible does not even include the word visualization (nor does it include the word trinity, or rapture, or a number of other doctrines that Christians hold dear). No one can find a verse of Scripture that says "Thou shalt visualize," nor can anyone find a verse of Scripture that says, "Thou shalt not visualize." Therefore, we will have to interpret some basic Bible principles to help give us an idea of what to believe. However, since there is not a precise command on the issue, we may do well to allow others liberty to apply a variety of biblical princiles in a variety of ways, and not force them to accept our personal interpretations of Scripture as the last word. If it were absolutely critical that we all totally agree on this issue and walk a precise line, I know that the Lord would have spoken very clearly regarding it.

As with every emerging truth, there have been misunderstandings, poor communication, and less than perfect comprehension of the evolving revelation. In the midst of this situation, we, the Church, must not be among those who come against; for we are called to be comforters, encouragers, edifiers, teachers, exhorters. These are the people who are needed today. People who, like the Holy Spirit, will come alongside and comfort and strengthen, and assist in clarification and definition of that which needs to be said. It is my desire to be one of these people. I challenge you to join these ranks.

I think that today the Church needs to teach its people, very pointedly and practically, how to begin to clearly and easily hear God's voice. In this way we will be able to reason in God's presence. We will be able to talk things over with God, and come away speaking His thoughts, rather than merely the reasonings of our own minds.

Secondly, I think that today we need to teach the Church, very pointedly and practically, how to begin to receive God's vision clearly and easily. Our sons and our daughters should be prophesying. Our young men should be seeing visions. Our old men should be dreaming dreams (Acts 2:17). Who will learn enough of the ways of the Spirit to instruct the Church as to how to live in these spiritual realities? **Or must we go on, blind and unhearing?**

God has given me a commission to dedicate my life to instructing the Church as to how Christians may live in these biblically promised spiritual realities of dream, vision, and God's spoken word within their hearts. As I present weekend **Communion With God** seminars all across the United

States and Canada, I find that church after church begins to move freely, easily, and naturally in hearing God's voice and seeing His vision.*

The mandate of the hour is to restore the knowledge of how to flow in the Spirit, using BOTH our reasoning capacity AND our visioning capacity. May each one assume his portion of this responsibility. May we together fulfill this mandate so that the Church may experience all that God has provided for her.

ANOTHER TESTIMONY CONCERNING VISION

In a recent seminar which I was conducting in Cincinnati, Ohio, I taught on vision briefly and then asked the participants to spend some time praying and asking God about using the eyes of their hearts to encounter Him. Let me share the following response from Rev. Stan Peters, President of the Greater Cincinnati School of the Bible.

"Lord, what about the eyes of my heart? How important is this to You and me — to our relationship and our walk together?"

God's response was..."Ask a blind man if he would like to see the robin he can hear? Ask him if he would like to see his mother, his father, his sweetheart?

"I tell you he will scream and shout and tell you he wants to see!

"You too need to be healed, just as the physically blind, and be able to see Me clearly so that we can walk in perfect union and love. How can two walk together unless they agree? Do you agree you want to see?"

Stan's response was "Yes, Lord!" To which the Lord replied, "Then you will! I love you, Stan."

* See information at the end of this book for ordering **Communion With God** training materials which you may use in training your church to begin flowing freely and naturally in Divine dream, vision, and dialogue with God.

BECOMING EXPRESSIONS OF GOD

By Mark Virkler

In this section of the book we want to explore the **positive** aspect of what it means to be **"In Christ."** The Bible has much to teach concerning becoming dead to self and alive to Christ. It is one of the central themes in the New Testament.

Following you will find a computer printout of 107 verses that speak of this great truth. I encourage you to study them carefully and prayerfully, asking God to give you a spirit of revelation so that the eyes of your heart may be enlightened (Eph. 1:17,18). Here are some questions for which you may want to seek answers.

1. What does it mean to be in Christ?
2. What does it mean to have Christ in me?
3. What does it mean to be joined to Christ (I Cor. 6:17)?
4. What does it mean to receive the Divine nature (II Pet. 1:4)?
5. What does it mean to be clothed with Christ (Gal. 3:27)?
6. What does it mean to have Christ formed within (Gal. 4:19)?
7. What does it mean to be strengthened with power through His Spirit in the inner man . . . (Eph. 3:16)?
8. What does it mean to be filled up with all the fullness of God (Eph. 3:19)?
9. What does it mean to grow up into all aspects into Him, who is the head, even Christ (Eph. 4:13)?

Allow the Holy Spirit to teach you as you ponder the Scriptures, seeking revelation knowledge about the **positive** teaching concerning the gift of **Christ's life** as revealed in the Word of God.

At the close of this section you will find some of my own thoughts concerning these truths. God's blessings as you study.

Index: **UNION (107 References)**
Title: *Becoming Expressions of God*
Range: **ACTS 1:1 to REVELATION 22:21**

ACT 17:28 For in him we live, and move, and have our being; as certain also of your own poets have said, For we are also his offspring.

ROM 8:1 (There is) therefore now no condemnation to them which are in Christ Jesus, who walk not after the flesh, but after the Spirit.
      2 For the law of the Spirit of life in Christ Jesus hath made me free from the law of sin and death.

ROM 12:5 So we, (being) many, are one body in Christ, and every one members one of another.

1 CO 1:2 Unto the church of God which is at Corinth, to them that are sanctified in Christ Jesus, called (to be) saints, with all that in every place call upon the name of Jesus Christ our Lord, both theirs and ours:

1 CO 1:30 But of him are ye in Christ Jesus, who of God is made unto us wisdom, and righteousness, and sanctification, and redemption:
      31 That, according as it is written, He that glorieth, let him glory in the Lord.

1 CO 2:1 And I, brethren, when I came to you, came not with excellency of speech or of wisdom, declaring unto you the testimony of God.
      2 For I determined not to know any thing among you, save Jesus Christ, and him crucified.
      3 And I was with you in weakness, and in fear, and in much trembling.
      4 And my speech and my preaching (was) not with enticing words of man's wisdom, but in demonstration of the Spirit and of power:
      5 That your faith should not stand in the wisdom of men, but in the power of God.
      6 Howbeit we speak wisdom among them that are perfect: yet not the wisdom of this world, nor of the princes of this world, that come to nought:
      7 But we speak the wisdom of God in a mystery, (even) the hidden (wisdom), which God ordained before the world unto our glory:
      8 Which none of the princes of this world knew: for had they known (it), they would not have crucified the Lord of glory.
      9 But as it is written, Eye hath not seen, nor ear heard, neither have entered into the heart of man, the things which God hath pre-

pared for them that love him.

10 But God hath revealed (them) unto us by the Spirit: for the Spirit searcheth all things, yea, the deep things of God.

11 For what man knoweth the things of a man, save the spirit of man which is in him? even so the things of God knoweth no man, but the Spirit of God.

12 Now we have received, not the Spirit of the world, but the Spirit which is of God; that we might know the things that are freely given to us of God.

13 Which things also we speak, not in the words which man's wisdom teacheth, but which the Holy Ghost teacheth; comparing spiritual things with spiritual.

14 But the natural man receiveth not the things of the Spirit of God: for they are foolishness unto him: neither can he know (them), because they are spiritually discerned.

15 But he that is spiritual judgeth all things, yet he himself is judged of no man.

16 For who hath known the mind of the Lord, that he may instruct him? But we have the mind of Christ.

1 CO 3:21 Therefore let no man glory in men. For all things are yours;

22 Whether Paul, or Apollos, or Cephas, or the world, or life, or death, or things present, or things to come; all are yours;

23 And ye are Christ's; and Christ (is) God's.

1 CO 6:17 But he that is joined unto the Lord is one Spirit.

1 CO 6:19 What? know ye not that your body is the temple of the Holy Ghost (which is) in you, which ye have of God, and ye are not your own?

1 CO 12:1 Now concerning spiritual (gifts), brethren, I would not have you ignorant.

2 Ye know that ye were Gentiles, carried away unto these dumb idols, even as ye were led.

3 Wherefore I give you to understand, that no man speaking by the Spirit of God calleth Jesus accursed: and (that) no man can say that Jesus is the Lord, but by the Holy Ghost.

4 Now there are diversities of gifts, but the same Spirit.

5 And there are differences of administrations, but the same Lord.

6 And there are diversities of operations, but it is the same God which worketh all in all.

7 But the manifestation of the Spirit is given to every man to profit withal.

1 CO 15:22 For as in Adam all die, even so in Christ shall all be made alive.

2 CH 1:21 Now he which stablisheth us with you in Christ, and hath anointed us, (is) God;

2 CH 5:17 Therefore if any man (be) in Christ, (he is) a new creature: old things are passed away; behold, all things are become new.

2 CH 5:21 For he hath made him (to be) sin for us, who knew no sin; that we might be made the righteousness of God in Him.

GAL 3:27 For as many of you as have been baptized into Christ have put on Christ.
    28 There is neither Jew nor Greek, there is neither bond nor free, there is neither male nor female: for ye are all one in Christ Jesus.

GAL 4:19 My little children, of whom I travail in birth again until Christ be formed in you.

EPH 1:3 Blessed (be) the God and Father of our Lord Jesus Christ, who hath blessed us with all spiritual blessings in heavenly (places) in Christ:

EPH 1:10 That in the dispensation of the fullness of times he might gather together in one all things in Christ, both which are in heaven, and which are on earth; (even) in him:
    11 In whom also we have obtained an inheritance, being predestinated according to the purpose of him who worketh all things after the counsel of his own will:

EPH 1:17 That the God of our Lord Jesus Christ, the Father of glory, may give unto you the spirit of wisdom and revelation in the knowledge of him:
    18 The eyes of your understanding being enlightened; that ye may know what is the hope of his calling, and what the riches of the glory of his inheritance in the saints,
    19 And what (is) the exceeding greatness of his power to us-ward who believe, according to the working of his mighty power,
    20 Which he wrought in Christ, when he raised him from the dead, and set (him) at his own right hand in the heavenly (places),
    21 Far above all principality, and power, and might, and dominion, and every name that is named, not only in this world, but also in that which is to come:
    22 And hath put all (things) under his feet, and gave him (to be)

the head over all (things) to the church,
23 Which is his body, the fullness of him that filleth all in all.

EPH 2:6 And hath raised (us) up together, and made (us) sit together in heavenly (places) in Christ Jesus:

EPH 2:13 But now in Christ Jesus ye who sometimes were far off are made nigh by the blood of Christ.

EPH 2:21 In whom all the building fitly framed together groweth unto an holy temple in the Lord:
22 In whom ye also are builded together for an habitation of God through the Spirit.

EPH 3:6 That the Gentiles should be fellowheirs, and of the same body, and partakers of his promise in Christ by the gospel:

EPH 3:12 In whom we have boldness and access with confidence by the faith of him.

EPH 3:19 And to know the love of Christ, which passeth knowledge, that ye might be filled with all the fullness of God.

PHI 3:9 And be found in him, not having mine own righteousness, which is of the law, but that which is through the faith of Christ, the righteousness which is of God by faith:

PHI 4:19 But my God shall supply all your need according to his riches in the glory by Christ Jesus.

COL 1:15 Who is the image of the invisible God, the firstborn of every creature:
16 For by him were all things created, that are in heaven, and that are in earth, visible and invisible, whether (they be) thrones, or dominions, or principalities, or powers: all things were created by him, and for him:
17 And he is before all things, and by him all things consist.
18 And he is the head of the body, the church: who is the beginning, the firstborn from the dead; that in all (things) he might have the preeminence.
19 For it pleased (the Father) that in him should all fullness dwell;

COL 1:26 (Even) the mystery which hath been hid from ages and from generations, but now is made manifest to his saints:

27 To whom God would make known what (is) the riches of the glory of this mystery among the Gentiles; which is Christ in you, the hope of glory:

28 Whom we preach, warning every man, and teaching every man in all wisdom; that we may present every man perfect in Christ Jesus:

29 Whereunto I also labour, striving according to his working, which worketh in me mightily.

COL 2:2 That their hearts might be comforted, being knit together in love, and unto all riches of the full assurance of understanding, to the acknowledgement of the mystery of God, and of the Father, and of Christ;

3 In whom are hid all the treasures of wisdom and knowledge.

COL 2:6 As ye have therefore received Christ Jesus the Lord, (so) walk ye in him:

7 Rooted and built up in him, and stablished in the faith, as ye have been taught, abounding therein with thanksgiving.

8 Beware lest any man spoil you through philosophy and vain deceit, after the tradition of men, after the rudiments of the world, and not after Christ.

9 For in him dwelleth all the fullness of the Godhead bodily.

10 And ye are complete in him, which is the head of all principality and power:

COL 2:11 In whom also ye are circumcised with the circumcision made without hands, in putting off the body of the sins of the flesh by the circumcision of Christ:

12 Buried with him in baptism, wherein also ye are risen with (him) through the faith of the operation of God, who hath raised him from the dead.

13 And you, being dead in your sins and the uncircumcision of your flesh, hath he quickened together with him, having forgiven you all trespasses;

14 Blotting out the handwriting of ordinances that was against us, which was contrary to us, and took it out of the way, nailing it to his cross;

15 (And) having spoiled principalities and powers, he made a shew of them openly, triumphing over them in it.

16 Let no man therefore judge you in meat, or in drink, or in respect of any holyday, or of the new moon, or of the sabbath (days):

17 Which are a shadow of things to come; but the body (is) of Christ.

18 Let no man beguile you of your reward in a voluntary humility and worshipping of angels, intruding into those things which he hath not seen, vainly puffed up by his fleshly mind,

19 And not holding the Head, from which all the body by joints and bands having nourishment ministered, and knit together, increaseth with the increase of God.

20 Wherefore if ye be dead with Christ from the rudiments of the world, why, as though living in the world, are ye subject to ordinances,

21 (Touch not; taste not; handle not;

22 Which all are to perish with the using;) after the commandments and doctrines of men?

23 Which things have indeed a shew of wisdom in will worship, and humility, and neglecting of the body; not in any honour to the satisfying of the flesh.

COL 3:1 If ye then be risen with Christ, seek those things which are above, where Christ sitteth on the right hand of God.

2 Set your affection on things above, not on things on the earth.

3 For ye are dead, and your life is hid with Christ in God.

COL 3:10 And have put on the new (man), which is renewed in knowledge after the image of him that created him:

11 Where there is neither Greek nor Jew, circumcision nor uncircumcision, Barbarian, Scythian, bond (nor) free: but Christ (is) all, and in all.

2 TI 2:1 Thou therefore, my son, be strong in the grace that is in Christ Jesus.

2 PE 1:4 Whereby are given unto us exceeding great and precious promises: that by these ye might be partakers of the divine nature, having escaped the corruption that is in the world through lust.

1 JO 4:7 Beloved, let us love one another: for love is of God; and every
· one that loveth is born of God, and knoweth God.

8 He that loveth not knoweth not God; for God is love.

9 In this was manifested the love of God toward us, because that God sent his only begotten Son into the world, that we might live through him.

10 Herein is love, not that we loved God, but that he loved us, and sent his Son (to be) the propitiation for our sins.

11 Beloved, if God so loved us, we ought also to love one another.

12 No man hath seen God at any time. If we love one another, God dwelleth in us, and his love is perfected in us.

13 Hereby know we that we dwell in him, and he in us, because he hath given us of his Spirit.

14 And we have seen and do testify that the Father sent the Son (to be) the Saviour of the world.

15 Whosoever shall confess that Jesus is the Son of God, God dwelleth in him, and he in God.

16 And we have known and believed the love that God hath to us. God is love; and he that dwelleth in love dwelleth in God, and God in him.

MY PERSONAL REFLECTIONS ON "CHRIST, MY LIFE"

By Mark Virkler

It took years for me as a Christian to become even partially conscious of what it meant for me to be in Christ. I have now written much on it in my study manual, **Abiding in Christ.** I will not repeat all of my earlier conclusions or proofs at this time but will only recap a few points, encouraging the interested student to read the **Abiding in Christ Study Manual and the Abiding in Christ Teacher's Guide.**

1. Through the work of salvation, God has removed the satanic nature (we **were** by **nature** children of **wrath** Eph. 2:2,3), and implanted within us the **Divine Nature** ("you might become partakers of the divine nature . . ." II Pet. 1:4).

2. We have died in Christ and come alive as a new kind of person (Gal. 2:20):

    a. Christ's Spirit is fused to ours (I Cor. 6:17).
    b. Christ is formed within (Gal. 4:19).
    c. We are clothed with Christ (Gal. 3:27).
    d. We live by His power (Phil. 4:19; Eph. 3:16,20).
    e. He has become our life (Col 3:4).
    f. He is our wisdom, righteousness, sanctification, and redemption (1 Cor. 1:30,31).
    g. His giftedness flows through us (1 Cor. 12:7-11).
    h. His character flows through us (Gal. 5:28-30).
    i. We have the mind of Christ (1 Cor. 2:16).
    j. We speak the "Oracles of God" (1 Pet. 4:11).
    k. We do His works (Jn. 14:12).

    Because of the fusion of the Holy Spirit to man's spirit (1 Cor. 6:17), in many aspects the two have become one, especially as we live tuned to the divine initiative as Jesus did through seeing in the spirit and hearing the voice of God in our hearts (Jn. 5:19, 20, 30; 8:26, 28, 38).

3. Our life in Christ is very different than satan's temptation of Eve to live as a god, because our position is arrived at through **dependent living** rather than the **independent living** that satan tempted Eve to establish. We do not seek to become gods. Instead, we offer our lives on the altar as a living sacrifice, and the **gift** God gives us in return is participation in His life, allowing us to become **expressions of Him. As dependent beings** (i.e. branches grafted into the vine) we have become **expressions of God to our world today.** Christ goes on living through His Church today.

4. In his commentary on the Epistle to the Galatians, Luther daringly
    stated: "The Christian is Christ." Ignatius wrote: "Christ is our in-
    separable life." Thomas Aquinas said that Christ and the Christians
    are "quasi one mystical person." The Scottish Catechism (Craig's)
    teaches: "Christ is not another person from His people properly."

5. The following pages from my **Abiding in Christ Study Manual**
    reflect more considerations on this subject.

CHRIST IN YOU

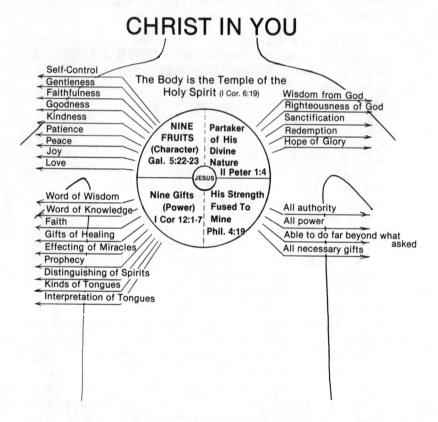

Filled up with the fullness of God (Eph 3:19)

Striving according to His Power which works mightily within me (Col.
1:29)

All things belong to you, You belong to Christ, Christ belongs to God
(I Cor. 3:21-23)

BEING IN CHRIST (EPH. 1-3)

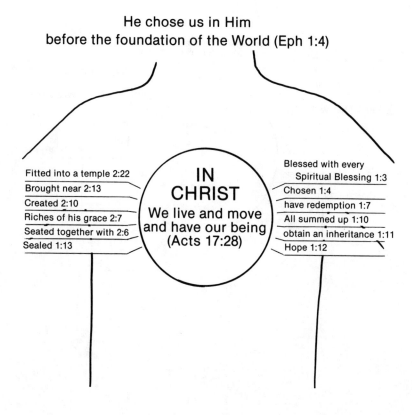

He chose us in Him
before the foundation of the World (Eph 1:4)

IN CHRIST
We live and move
and have our being
(Acts 17:28)

Fitted into a temple 2:22

Brought near 2:13

Created 2:10

Riches of his grace 2:7

Seated together with 2:6

Sealed 1:13

Blessed with every
Spiritual Blessing 1:3

Chosen 1:4

have redemption 1:7

All summed up 1:10

obtain an inheritance 1:11

Hope 1:12

In Christ we have obtained an inheritance (Eph 1:11)
Christ is all and in all (Col. 3:11)

SENSING GOD WITHIN

(These are examples of the Holy Spirit within man's spirit.)

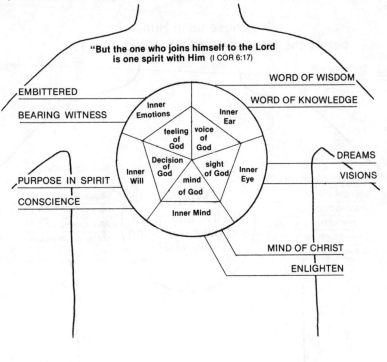

"The spirit of man is the lamp of the Lord, searching the innermost parts of his being (Prov 20:27)

"The lamp of your body is your eye, when your eye is clear, your whole body is full of light; but when it is bad, your body also is filled with darkness.

Then watch out that the light in you may not be darkness." (LK 11:34-35)

HOW THE SPIRIT IS STRENGTHENED:
PREGNANT WITH VISION & RHEMA

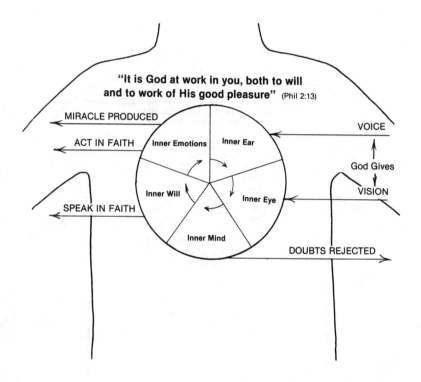

"Pray to be strengthened with power through His spirit in the inner man so that Christ may dwell in your heart by faith, that you may be able to comprehend the unbelievable dimensions of the love of Christ which surpasses all knowledge that you might be filled up to all the fullness of God."
(Eph 3:14-19 paraphrased)

THE DAY DAWNS—
THE MORNING STAR ARISES IN OUR HEARTS

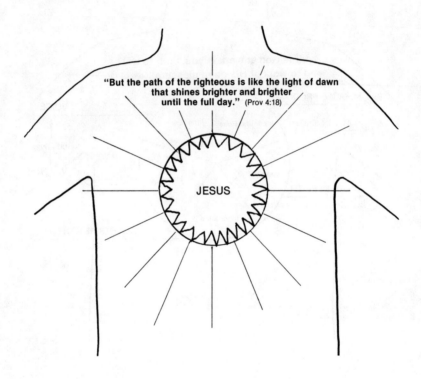

"But the path of the righteous is like the light of dawn
that shines brighter and brighter
until the full day." (Prov 4:18)

JESUS

"Let us pay attention to the prophetic word made sure as to a lamp shining in a dark place, until the day dawns and the morning star arises in our hearts." (II Pet 1:19)

POSITIVE MENTAL ATTITUDE AND THE WORD OF GOD

Again the best way to see where God stands on a subject is to study as many verses in the Bible as possible on that topic. Using CompuBIBLE we have gathered together 363 verses that demonstrate the positive things God has to say about having a positive mental attitude. As you study through these verses you will see that God is incurably optimistic and commands us to be also. The verses listed deal with commands to rejoice, be thankful, and optimistic under all circumstances, as well as providing many examples of men and women who did so. As you study these verses, build your own theology concerning God's wishes about our mental attitude. Allow God to speak to you as you study. Following are some questions for which you may want to discover answers.

1. Would God Himself be characterized as one who has a positive mental attitude?

2. What are God's commands concerning the kind of mental attitude we are supposed to exhibit?

3. What are the examples of the great men of the Bible concerning the kinds of mental attitudes they held?

4. What should be our mental attitudes when things appear to be going wrong?

5. What is God's view of grumblers?

As you go through the following concordance study, feel free to add other verses which we may have missed. Allow God the opportunity to disclose to you the kind of thought processes He is seeking to instill in your mind, and how they are different than those of the world. At the end of this section you will find some of my own thoughts concerning this subject. Lord, Open our hearts and minds to your Word as we study.

Index: JOY (287 References)
Title: *A Positive Mental Attitude and the Word of God*
Range: *GENESIS 1:1 to Revelation 22:21*
Subject —
1. rejoice
2. thank
3. bless
4. joy
5. glad

We have broken the following verses down into 7 categories to facilitate your study. They are:

1. Institutions of Praise, Worship and Thanksgiving God Has Created.
2. Commands and Exhortations to Be Thankful and Give Praise.
3. Commands (and Examples) to Be Thankful Even in Adversity.
4. Examples of People in The Bible Who Were Thankful.
5. Consequences of Not Being Thankful.
6. Results of Praise and Thankfulness.
7. Joy and Gladness Originate in God.

AREA ONE — INSTITUTIONS OF PRAISE, WORSHIP AND THANKSGIVING GOD HAS CREATED

Examine the following verses to discover how God established a number of institutions (feasts, etc.) in which His people were to praise and give thanks. I am amazed at the great variety of feasts that God established in which the Israelites were commanded to express a positive mental and spiritual attitude. This attitude was to be central to their lives. Not only is in central to mankind's life, it is also the requirement and response of nature. "The floods clap their hands, the hills are joyful together, the fir trees rejoice in God." Praise, worship and rejoicing are absolutely central to all of life. A positive mental and spiritual attitude is where it's at for all the world.

LEV 22:29 And when ye will offer a sacrifice of thanksgiving unto the Lord, offer (it) at your own will.

LEV 23:40 And ye shall take you on the first day the boughs of goodly trees, branches of palm trees, and the boughs of thick trees, and willows of the brook; and ye shall rejoice before the Lord your God seven days.

DEU 14:24 And if the way be too long for thee, so that thou art not able to carry it; (or) if the place be too far from thee, which the Lord thy God shall choose to set his name there, when the Lord thy God hath blessed thee:

25 Then shalt thou turn (it) into money, and bind up the money in thine hand, and shalt go unto the place which the Lord thy God shall choose:

26 And thou shalt bestow that money for whatsoever thy soul lusteth after, for oxen, or for sheep, or for wine, or for strong drink, or for whatsoever thy soul desireth: and thou shalt eat there before the Lord thy God, and thou shalt rejoice, thou, and thine household.

DUE 16:10 And thou shalt keep the feast of weeks unto the Lord thy God with a tribute of a freewill offering of thine hand, which thou shalt give (unto the Lord thy God), according as the Lord thy God hath blessed thee:

11 And thou shalt rejoice before the Lord thy God, thou, and thy son, and thy daughter, and thy manservant, and thy maidservant, and the Levite that (is) within thy gates, and the stranger, and the fatherless, and the widow, that (are) among you, in the place which the Lord thy God hath chosen to place his name there.

DEU 16:14 And thou shalt rejoice in thy feast, thou, and thy son, and thy daughter, and thy manservant, and thy maidservant, and the Levite, the stranger, and the fatherless, and the widow, that (are) within thy gates.

DEU 27:7 And thou shalt offer peace offerings, and shalt eat there, and rejoice before the Lord thy God.

1 CH 23:30 And to stand every morning to thank and praise the Lord, and likewise at even:

1 CH 25:3 Of Jeduthum: the sons of Jeduthun; Gedaliah, and Zeri, and Jeshaiah, Hashabiah, and Mattithiah, six, under the hands of their father Jeduthun, who prophesied with a harp, to give thanks and to praise the Lord.

NEH 12:8 Moreover the Levites: Jeshua, Binnui, Kadmiel, Sherebiah, Judah, (and) Mattaniah, (which was) over the thanksgiving, he and his brethren.

PSA 96:11 Let the heavens rejoice, and let the earth be glad; let the sea roar, and the fullness thereof.

12 Let the field be joyful, and all that (is) therein: then shall all the trees of the wood rejoice.

PSA 97:1 The Lord reigneth; let the earth rejoice; let the multitude of isles be glad (thereof).

PSA 98:8 Let the floods clap (their) hands: let the hills be joyful together.

ISA 14:7 The whole earth is at rest, (and) is quiet: they break forth into singing.
8 Yea, the fir trees rejoice at thee, (and) the cedars of Lebanon, (saying), Since thou art laid down, no feller is come up against us.

ZEC 8:19 Thus saith the Lord of hosts; The fast of the fourth (month), and the fast of the fifth, and the fast of the seventh, and the fast of the tenth, shall be to the house of Judah joy and gladness, and cheerful feasts; therefore love and truth and peace.

AREA TWO — COMMANDS AND EXHORTATIONS TO BE THANKFUL AND GIVE PRAISE

Notice how often God, and David, and others **command** us to praise, and give thanks. Praise and thanks is not optional, nor is it given when we feel like it. We are to praise on command of the King! We worship by command! You find this stated over and over. What a revolutionizing concept. We do not worship when we feel like it. We worship by command of the King. Not only was this worship and praise to be continuous, it was to be exuberant. "Shout for joy" is a common description for it. Therefore let us forever be glad and rejoice, and give honour to Him, and put away forever a negative mental and spiritual attitude.

DEU 8:10 When thou hast eaten and art full, then thou shalt bless the Lord thy God for the good land which he hath given thee.

DEU 12:7 And there ye shall eat before the Lord your God, and ye shall rejoice in all that ye put your hand unto, ye and your households, wherein the Lord thy God hath blessed thee.

DEU 12:12 And ye shall rejoice before the Lord your God, ye, and your sons, and your daughters, and your menservants, and your maidservants, and the Levite that (is) within your gates; forasmuch as he hath no part nor inheritance with you.

DEU 12:18 But thou must eat them before the Lord thy God in the place which the Lord thy God shall choose, thou, and thy son, and thy daughter, and thy manservant, and thy maidservant, and the Levite that (is) within thy gates: and thou shalt rejoice before the Lord thy God in all that thou puttest thine hands unto.

DEU 26:11 And thou shalt rejoice in every good (thing) which the Lord thy God hath given unto thee, and unto thine house, thou, and the Levite, and the stranger that (is) among you.

1 CH 15:16 And David spake to the chief of the Levites to appoint their brethren (to be) the singers with instruments of musick, psalteries and harps and cymbals, sounding, by lifting up the voice with joy.

1 CH 16:4 And he appointed (certain) of the Levites to minister before the ark of the Lord, and to record, and to thank and praise the Lord God of Israel:

1 CH 16:8 Give thanks unto the Lord, call upon his name, make known his deeds among the people.
     9 Sing unto him, sing psalms unto him, talk ye of all his wondrous works.
     10 Glory ye in his holy name: let the heart of them rejoice that seek the Lord.
     11 Seek the Lord and his strength, seek his face continually.
     12 Remember his marvelous works that he hath done, his wonders, and the judgements of his mouth;
     13 O ye seed of Israel his servant, ye children of Jacob, his chosen ones.
     14 He (is) the Lord our God; his judgements (are) in all the earth.
     15 Be ye mindful always of his covenant; the word (which) he commanded to a thousand generations;

2 CH 29:30 Moreover Hezekiah the king and the princes commanded the Levites to sing praise unto the Lord with the words of David, and of Asaph the seer. And they sang praises with gladness, and they bowed their heads and worshipped.
     31 Then Hezekiah answered and said, Now ye have consecrated yourselves unto the Lord, come near and bring sacrifices and thank offerings into the house of the Lord. And the congregation brought in sacrifices and thank offerings; and as many as were of a free heart burnt offerings.

2 CH 31:2 And Hezekiah appointed the courses of the priests and the Levites after their courses, every man according to his service, the priests and Levites for burnt offerings and for peace offerings, to minister, and to give thanks, and to praise in the gates of the tents of the Lord.

NEH 9:5 Then the Levites, Jeshua, and Kadmiel, Bani, Hashabniah, Sherebiah, Hodijah, Shebaniah, (and) Pethahiah, said, Stand up (and) bless the Lord your God for ever and ever: and blessed be thy glorious name, which is exalted above all blessing and praise.

NEH 12:24 And the chief of the Levites: Hashabiah, Sherebiah, and Jeshua the son of Kadmiel, with their brethren over against them, to praise (and) to give thanks, according to the commandment of David the man of God, ward over against ward.
    27 And at the dedication of the wall of Jerusalem they sought the Levites out of all their places, to bring them to Jerusalem, to keep the dedication with gladness, both with thanksgivings, and with singing, (with) cymbals, psalteries, and with harps.
    31 Then I brought up the princes of Judah upon the wall, and appointed two great (companies of them that gave) thanks, (whereof one) went on the right hand upon the wall toward the dung gate:
    38 And the other (company of them that gave) thanks went over against (them), and I after them, and the half of the people upon the wall, from beyond the tower of the furnaces even unto the broad wall;
    40 So stood the two (companies of them that gave) thanks in the house of God, and I, and the half of the rulers with me:
    43 Also that day they offered great sacrifices, and rejoiced: for God had made them rejoice with great joy: the wives also and the children rejoiced: so that the joy of Jerusalem was heard even afar off.
    46 For in the days of David and Asaph of old (there were) chief of the singers, and songs of praise and thanksgiving unto God.

PSA 30:4 Sing unto the Lord, O ye saints of his, and give thanks at the remembrance of his holiness.
    5 For his anger (endureth but) a moment; in his favour (is) life: weeping may endure for a night, but joy (cometh) in the morning.

PSA 32:11 Be glad in the Lord, and rejoice, ye righteous: and shout for joy, all (ye that are) upright in heart.

PSA 33:1 Rejoice in the Lord, O ye righteous: (for) praise is comely for the upright.

2 Praise the Lord with harp: sing unto him with the psaltery and (an) instrument of ten strings.

3 Sing unto him a new song; play skillfully with a loud noise.

PSA 81:1 Sing aloud unto God our strength: make a joyful noise unto the God of Jacob.

PSA 96:2 Sing unto the Lord, bless his name; shew forth his salvation from day to day.

PSA 103:22 Bless the Lord, all his works in all places of his dominion: bless the Lord, O my soul.

PSA 104:1 Bless the Lord, O my soul. O Lord my God, thou art very great: thou art clothed with honour and majesty.

PSA 107:31 Oh that (men) would praise the Lord (for) his goodness, and (for) his wonderful works to the children of men!

32 Let them exalt him also in the congregation of the people, and praise him in the assembly of the elders.

PSA 108:7 God hath spoken in his holiness; I will rejoice, I will divide Shechem, and mete out the valley of Succoth.

PSA 118:24 This (is) the day (which) the Lord hath made; we will rejoice and be glad in it.

29 O give thanks unto the Lord; for (he is) good: for his mercy (endureth) forever.

PSA 134:1 Behold, bless ye the Lord, all (ye) servants of the Lord, which by night stand in the house of the Lord.

2 Lift up your hands (in) the sanctuary, and bless the Lord.

PSA 135:1 Praise ye the Lord. Praise ye the name of the Lord; praise (him), O ye servants of the Lord.

2 Ye that stand in the house of the Lord, in the courts of the house of our God.

3 Praise the Lord; for the Lord (is) good: sing praises unto his name; for (it is) pleasant.

PSA 135:19 Bless the Lord, O house of Israel: bless the Lord, O house of Aaron:

20 Bless the Lord, O house of Levi: ye that fear the Lord, bless the Lord.

21 Blessed be the Lord out of Zion, which dwelleth at Jerusalem. Praise ye the Lord.

PSA 136:1 O give thanks unto the Lord; for (he is) good: for his mercy (endureth) forever.
    2 O give thanks unto God of gods: for his mercy (endureth) forever.
    3 O give thanks to the Lord of lords: for his mercy (endureth) forever.

PSA 136:26 O give thanks unto the God of heaven: for his mercy (endureth) forever.

PSA 145:21 My mouth shall speak the praise of the Lord: and let all flesh bless his holy name forever and ever.

PSA 147:7 Sing unto the Lord with thanksgiving; sing praise upon the harp unto our God:

PSA 149:5 Let the saints be joyful in glory; let them sing aloud upon their beds.

PROV 5:18 Let thy fountain be blessed: and rejoice with the wife of thy youth.

ISA 66:10 Rejoice ye with Jerusalem, and be glad with her, all ye that love her: rejoice for joy with her, all ye that mourn for her:

ZEPH 3:14 Sing, O daughter of Zion; shout, O Israel; be glad and rejoice with all the heart, O daughter of Jerusalem.

EPH 5:4 Neither filthiness, nor foolish talking, nor jesting, which are not convenient: but rather giving of thanks.

PHI 3:1 Finally, my brethren, rejoice in the Lord. To write the same things to you, to me indeed (is) not grievous, but for you (it is) safe.

COL 3:15 And let the peace of God rule in your hearts, to the which also ye are called in one body; and be ye thankful.

COL 3:17 And whatsoever ye do in word or deed, (do) all in the name of the Lord Jesus, giving thanks to God and the Father by him.

COL 4:2 Continue in prayer, and watch in the same with thanksgiving;

1 TH 5:18 In everything give thanks: for this is the will of God in Christ Jesus concerning you.

1 TI 2:1 I exhort therefore, that, first of all, supplications, prayers, inter- cessions, (and) giving of thanks, be made for all men;

HEB 13:15 By him therefore let us offer the sacrifice of praise to God continually, that is, the fruit of (our) lips giving thanks to his name.

REV 19:7 Let us be glad and rejoice, and give honour to him: for the marriage of the Lamb is come, and his wife hath made herself ready.

AREA THREE — COMMANDS (AND EXAMPLES) TO BE THANKFUL EVEN IN ADVERSITY

Examine the following verses and discover what our mental and spiritual attitude is to be when things are not going well. Are we allowed to ever become negative or must a positive mental and spiritual attitude go with us wherever we are? You will find that we are under command to **always** have a positive mental attitude.

JOB 1:21 And said, Naked came I out of my mother's womb, and naked shall I return thither: the Lord gave, and the Lord hath taken away; blessed be the name of the Lord.

PSA 27:6 And now shall mine head be lifted up above mine enemies round about me: therefore will I offer his tabernacle sacrifices of joy; I will sing, yea, I will sing praises unto the Lord.

PSA 31:7 I will be glad and rejoice in thy mercy: for thou hast considered my trouble; thou hast known my soul in adversities;

PSA 34:1 I will bless the Lord at all times: his praise (shall) continually (be) in my mouth.
    2 My soul shall make her boast in the Lord: the humble shall hear (thereof), and be glad.

ISA 49:13 Sing, O heavens; and be joyful, O earth; and break forth into singing, O mountains: for the Lord hath comforted his people, and will have mercy upon his afflicted.

ISA 51:3 For the Lord shall comfort Zion: he will comfort all her waste places; and he will make her wilderness like Eden, and her desert like the garden of the Lord; joy and gladness shall be found therein, thanks-giving, and the voice of melody.

ISA 52:9 Break forth into joy, sing together, ye waste places of Jersalem: for the Lord hath comforted his people, he hath redeemed Jerusalem.

MAT 5:12 Rejoice, and be exceeding glad: for great (is) your reward in heaven: for so persecuted they the prophets which were before you.

MAT 5:44 But I say unto you, Love your enemies, bless them that curse you, do good to them that hate you, and pray for them which despite-fully use you, and persecute you;

LUK 6:22 Blessed are ye when men shall hate you, and when they shall separate you (from their company), and shall reproach (you), and cast out your name as evil, for the Son of man's sake.
    23 Rejoice ye in that day, and leap for joy: for, behold, your re-ward (is) great in heaven: for in the like manner did their fathers unto the prophets.

ROM 12:14 Bless them which persecute you: bless, and curse not.

1 CO 4:12 And labour, working with our own hands: being reviled, we bless; being persecuted, we suffer it:

2 CO 7:4 Great (is) my boldness of speech toward you, great (is) my glorying of you: I am filled with comfort, I am exceeding joyful in all our tribulation.

2 CO 8:2 How that in a great trial of affliction the abundance of their joy and their deep poverty abounded unto the riches of their liberality.

2 CO 12:9 And he said unto me, My grace is sufficient for thee: for my strength is made perfect in weakness. Most gladly therefore will I rather glory in my infirmities, that the power of Christ may rest upon me.
    13 For we are glad, when we are weak, and ye are strong: and this also we wish, (even) your perfection.

COL 1:24 Who now rejoice in my sufferings for you, and fill up that which is behind the afflictions of Christ in my flesh for his body's sake, which is the church:

JAM 1:2 My brethren, count it all joy when ye fall into diverse tempta-tions;

JAM 1:9 Let the brother of low degree rejoice in that he is exalted:

AREA FOUR — EXAMPLES OF PEOPLE IN THE BIBLE WHO WERE THANKFUL

Notice in the following pages of verses that the Bible is full of testimonies of people who lived out a life of thanks and worship. For anyone to suggest that having a positive mental attitude is cultish is beyond my wildest imagination. It is not only ordained by God, it is shown by Scripture to be the only acceptable attitude that one may hold. God is not into negative mental attitudes.

1 SAM 2:1 And Hannah prayed, and said, My heart rejoiceth in the Lord, mine horn is exalted in the Lord: my mouth is enlarged over mine enemies; because I rejoice in thy salvation.

2 SAM 22:50 Therefore I will give thanks unto thee, O lord, among the heathen, and I will sing praises unto thy name.

1 KI 8:66 On the eighth day he sent the people away: and they blessed the king, and went unto their tents joyful and glad of heart for all the goodness that the Lord had done for David his servant, and for Israel his people.

1 CH 15:25 So David, and the elders of Israel, and the captains over thousands, went to bring up the ark of the covenant of the Lord out of the house of Obededom with joy.

1 CH 16:7 Then on that day David delivered first (this Psalm) to thank the Lord into the hand of Asaph and his brethren.

1 CH 16:31 Let the heavens be glad, and let the earth rejoice: and let (men) say among the nations, The Lord reigneth.

32 Let the sea roar, and the fullness thereof: let the fields rejoice, and all that (is) therein.

34 O give thanks unto the Lord; for (he is) good; for his mercy (endureth) forever.

35 And say ye, Save us, O God of our salvation, and gather us together, and deliver us from the heathen, that we may give thanks to thy holy name, (and) glory in thy praise.

36 Blessed (be) the Lord God of Israel forever and ever. And all the people said, Amen, and praised the Lord.

1 CH 16:41 And with them Heman and Jeduthun, and the rest that were chosen, who were expressed by name, to give thanks to the Lord, because his mercy (endureth) forever;

1 CH 29:9 Then the people rejoiced, for that they offered willingly, because with perfect heart they offered willingly to the Lord: and David the king also rejoiced with great joy.

1 CH 29:13 Now therefore, our God, we thank thee, and praise thy glorious name.

2 CH 6:41 Now therefore arise, O Lord God, into thy resting place, thou, and the ark of thy strength: let thy priests, O Lord God, be clothed with salvation, and let thy saints rejoice in goodness.

2 CH 7:10 And on the three and twentieth day of the seventh month he sent the people away into their tents, glad and merry in heart for the goodness that the Lord had shewed unto David, and to Solomon, and to Israel his people.

2 CH 30:21 And the children of Israel that were present at Jerusalem kept the feast of unleavened bread seven days with great gladness: and the Levites and the priests praised the Lord day by day, (singing) with loud instruments unto the Lord.

2 CH 30:23 And the whole assembly took counsel to keep other seven days: and they kept (other) seven days with gladness.

2 CH 30:26 So there was great joy in Jerusalem: for since the time of Solomon the son of David king of Israel (there was) not the like in Jerusalem.

2 CH 31:8 And when Hezekiah and the princes came and saw the heaps, they blessed the Lord, and his people Israel.

EZR 3:11 And they sang together by course in praising and giving thanks unto the Lord; because (he is) good, for his mercy (endureth) forever toward Israel. And all the people shouted with a great shout, when they praised the Lord, because the foundation of the house of the Lord was laid.
12 But many of the priests and Levites and chief of the fathers, (who were) ancient men, and had seen the first house, when the foundation of this house was laid before their eyes, wept with a loud voice; and many shouted aloud for joy:

13 So that the people could not discern the noise of the shout of joy from the noise of the weeping of the people: for the people shouted with a loud shout, and the noise was heard afar off.

EZR 6:16 And the children of Israel, the priests, and the Levites, and the rest of the children of the captivity, kept the dedication of this house of God with joy.

NEH 8:6 And Ezra blessed the Lord, the great God. And all the people answered, Amen, Amen, with lifting up their hands: and they bowed their heads, and worshipped the Lord with (their) faces to the ground.

NEH 8:17 And all the congregation of them that were come again out of the captivity made booths, and sat under the booths: for since the days of Jeshua the son of Nun unto that day had not the children of Israel done so. And there was very great gladness.

NEH 11:17 And Mattaniah the son of Micha, the son of Zabdi, the son of Asaph, (was) the principal to begin the thanksgiving in prayer: and Bakbukiah the second among his brethren and Abda the son of Shammua, the son of Galal, the son of Jeduthun.

PSA 5:11 But let all those that put their trust in thee rejoice: let them ever shout for joy, because thou defendest them: let them also that love thy name be joyful in thee.

PSA 9:2 I will be glad and rejoice in thee: I will sing praise to thy name, O thou most High.

PSA 9:14 That I may shew forth all thy praise in the gates of the daughter of Zion: I will rejoice in thy salvation.

PSA 13:5 But I have trusted in thy mercy; my heart shall rejoice in thy salvation.
6 I will sing unto the Lord, because he hath dealt bountifully with me.

PSA 16:7 I will bless the Lord, who hath given me counsel: my reins also instruct me in the night seasons.

PSA 16:9 Therefore my heart is glad, and my glory rejoiceth: my flesh also shall rest in hope.

PSA 18:46 The Lord liveth; and blessed (be) my rock; and let the God of my salvation be exalted.

PSA 18:49 Therefore will I give thanks unto thee, O Lord, among the heathen, and sing praises unto thy name.

PSA 20:5 We will rejoice in thy salvation, and in the name of our God we will set up (our) banners: the Lord fulfill all thy petitions.

PSA 21:1 The king shall joy in thy strength, O Lord; and in thy salvation how greatly shall he rejoice!

PSA 21:6 That I may publish with the voice of thanksgiving, and tell of all thy wondrous works.

PSA 26:12 My foot standeth in an even place: in the congregations will I bless the Lord.

PSA 33:21 For our heart shall rejoice in him, because we have trusted in his holy name.

PSA 35:9 And my soul shall be joyful in the Lord: it shall rejoice in his salvation.

PSA 35:18 I will give thee thanks in the great congregation: I will praise thee among much people.

PSA 40:16 Let all those that seek thee rejoice and be glad in thee: let such as love thy salvation say continually, The Lord be magnified.

PSA 43:4 Then will I go unto the altar of God, unto God my exceeding joy: yea, upon the harp will I praise thee, O God my God.

PSA 50:14 Offer unto God thanksgiving; and pay thy vows unto the most High:

PSA 63:4 Thus will I bless thee while I live: I will lift up my hands in thy name.
   5 My soul shall be satisfied as (with) marrow and fatness; and my mouth shall praise (thee) with joyful lips:
   6 When I remember thee upon my bed, (and) meditate on thee in the (night) watches.
   7 Because thou hast been my help, therefore in the shadow of thy wings will I rejoice.

PSA 64:10 The righteous shall be glad in the Lord, and shall trust in him; and all the upright in heart shall glory.

PSA 65:12 They drop (upon) the pastures of the wilderness: and the little hills rejoice on every side.
13 The pastures are clothed with flocks; the valleys also are covered over with corn; they shout for joy, they also sing.

PSA 66:1 Make a joyful noise unto God, all ye lands:
2 Sing forth the honour of his name: make his praise glorious.

PSA 66:4 All the earth shall worship thee, and shall sing unto thee; they shall sing (to) thy name. Selah.

PSA 66:8 O bless our God, ye people, and make the voice of his praise to be heard:

PSA 67:3 Let the people praise thee, O God; let all the people praise thee.
4 O let the nations be glad and sing for joy: for thou shalt judge the people righteously, and govern the nations upon earth. Selah.
5 Let the people praise thee, O God; let all the people praise thee.

PSA 68:3 But let the righteous be glad; let them rejoice before God: yea, let them exceedingly rejoice.
4 Sing unto God, sing praises to his name: extol him that rideth upon the heavens by his name JAH, and rejoice before him.

PSA 60:30 I will praise the name of God with a song, and will magnify him with thanksgiving.
31 (This) also shall please the Lord better than an ox (or) bullock that hath horns and hoofs.
32 The humble shall see (this, and) be glad: and your heart shall live that seek God.

PSA 70:4 Let all those that seek thee rejoice and be glad in thee: and let such as love thy salvation say continually, Let God be magnified.

PSA 71:23 My lips shall greatly rejoice when I sing unto thee; and my soul, which thou hast redeemed.

PSA 75:1 Unto thee, O God, do we give thanks, (unto thee) do we give thanks: for (that) thy name is near thy wondrous works declare.

PSA 79:13 So we thy people and sheep of thy pasture will give thee thanks forever: we will shew forth thy praise to all generations.

PSA 89:16 In thy name shall they rejoice all the day: and in thy right-eousness they shall be exalted.

PSA 97:8 Zion heard, and was glad; and the daughters of Judah rejoiced because of thy judgements, O Lord.

PSA 97:11 Light is sown for the righteous, and gladness for the upright in heart.
    12 Rejoice in the Lord, ye righteous; and give thanks at the re-membrance of his holiness.

PSA 98:4 Make a joyful noise unto the Lord, all the earth: make a loud noise, and rejoice, and sing praise.
    5 Sing unto the Lord with the harp; with the harp, and the voice of a psalm.
    6 With trumpets and sound of cornet make a joyful noice before the Lord, the king.

PSA 92:1 (It is a) good (thing) to give thanks unto the Lord, and to sing praises unto thy name, O most High:
    2 To shew forth thy loving kindness in the morning, and thy faith-fulness every night,
    3 Upon an instrument of ten strings, and upon the psaltery; upon the harp with a solemn sound.
    4 For thou, Lord, hast made me glad through thy work: I will tri-umph in the works of thy hands.

PSA 95:1 O come, let us sing unto the Lord: let us make a joyful noise to the rock of our salvation.
    2 Let us come before his presence with thanksgiving, and make a joyful noise unto him with psalms.

PSA 100:1 Make a joyful noise unto the Lord, all ye lands,
    2 Serve the Lord with gladness: come before his presence with singing.

PSA 100:4 Enter into his gates with thanksgiving, (and) into his courts with praise: be thankful unto him, (and) bless his name.

PSA 104:34 My meditation of him shall be sweet: I will be glad in the Lord.

PSA 105:1 O Give thanks unto the Lord; call upon his name: make known his deeds among the people.

PSA 105:3 Glory ye in his holy name: let the heart of them rejoice that seek the Lord.

PSA 106:1 Praise ye the Lord. O give thanks unto the Lord; for (he is) good: for his mercy (endureth) forever.

PSA 107:22 And let them sacrifice the sacrifices of thanksgiving, and declare his works with rejoicing.

PSA 115:18 But we will bless the Lord from this time forth and for evermore. Praise the Lord.

PSA 116:17 I will offer to thee the sacrifice of thanksgiving, and will call upon the name of the Lord.

PSA 118:1 O give thanks unto the Lord; for (he is) good: because his mercy (endureth) forever.

PSA 119:62 At midnight I will rise to give thanks unto thee because of thy righteous judgments.

PSA 119:162 I rejoice at thy word, as one that findeth great spoil.

PSA 140:13 Surely the righteous shall give thanks unto thy name: the upright shall dwell in thy presence.

PSA 145:1 I will extol thee, my God, O king; and I will bless thy name forever and ever.
   2 Every day will I bless thee; and I will praise thy name forever and ever.

PSA 145:10 All thy works shall praise thee, O Lord; and thy saints shall bless thee.

ISA 12:3 Therefore with joy shall ye draw water out of the wells of salvation.

ISA 13:3 I have commanded my sanctified ones, I have also called my mighty ones for mine anger, (even) them that rejoice in my highness.

ISA 29:19 The meek also shall increase (their) joy in the Lord, and the poor among men shall rejoice in the Holy One of Israel.

ISA 35:10 And the ransomed of the Lord shall return, and come to

Zion with songs and everlasting joy upon their heads: they shall obtain joy and gladness, and sorrow and sighing shall flee away.

JONA 2:9 But I will sacrifice unto thee with the voice of thanksgiving; I will pay (that) that I have vowed. Salvation (is) of the Lord.

HAB 3:18 Yet I will rejoice in the Lord, I will joy in the God of my salvation.

ACTS 2:46 And they, continuing daily with one accord in the temple, and breaking bread from house to house, did eat their meat with gladness and singleness of heart.

ROM 5:11 And not only (so), but we also joy in God through our Lord Jesus Christ, by whom we have now received the atonement.

2 CO 7:9 Now I rejoice, not that ye were made sorry, but that ye sorrowed to repentance: for ye were made sorry after a godly manner, that ye might receive damage by us in nothing.

EPH 1:16 Cease not to give thanks for you, making mention of you in my prayers;

EPH 5:20 Giving thanks always for all things unto God and the Father in the name of our Lord Jesus Christ;

PHI 1:3 I thank my God upon every remembrance of you,
    4 Always in every prayer of mine for you all making request with joy.

PHI 3:3 For we are the circumcision, which worship God in the spirit, and rejoice in Christ Jesus, and have no confidence in the flesh.

PHI 2:17 Yea, and if I be offered upon the sacrifice and service of your faith, I joy, and rejoice with you all.
    18 For the same cause also do ye joy, and rejoice with me.

PHI 4:6 Be careful for nothing; but in everything by prayer and supplication with thanksgiving let your requests be made known unto God.
    7 And the peace of God, which passeth all understanding, shall keep your hearts and minds through Christ Jesus.
    8 Finally, brethren, whatsoever things are true, whatsoever things (are) honest, whatsoever things (are) just, whatsoever things (are) pure, whatsoever things (are) lovely, whatsoever things (are) of good report;

if (there be) any virtue, and if (there be) any praise, think on these things.

COL 1:3 We give thanks to God and the Father of our Lord Jesus Christ, praying always for you.

COL 1:11 Strengthened with all might, according to his glorious power, unto all patience and long suffering with joyfulness;
    12 Giving thanks unto the Father, which hath made us meet to be partakers of the inheritance of the saints in light:

COL 2:5 For though I be absent in the flesh, yet am I with you in the spirit, joying and beholding your order, and the stedfastness of your faith in Christ.

COL 2:7 Rooted and built up in him, and stablished in the faith, as ye have been taught, abounding therein with thanksgiving.

1 TH 1:2 We give thanks to God always for you all, making mention of you in our prayers;

1 TH 2:13 For this cause also thank we God without ceasing, because, when ye received the word of God which ye heard of us, ye received (it) not (as) the word of men, but as it is in truth, the word of God, which effectually worketh also in you that believe.

2 TH 1:3 We are bound to thank God always for you, brethren, as it is meet, because that your faith groweth exceedingly, and the charity of everyone of you all toward each other aboundeth;
PHM 1:4 I thank my God, making mention of thee always in my prayers.

HEB 12:2 Looking unto Jesus the author and finisher of (our) faith; who for the joy that was set before him endured the cross, despising the shame, and is set down at the right hand of the throne of God.

1 PET 1:8 Whom having not seen, ye love; in whom, though now ye see (him) not, yet believing, ye rejoice with joy unspeakable and full of glory:

1 JOHN 1:4 And these things write we unto you, that your joy may be full.

2 JOHN 1:12 Having many things to write unto you, I would not (write)

with paper and ink: but I trust to come unto you, and speak face to face, that our joy may be full.

REV. 4:9 And when those beasts give glory and honour and thanks to him that sat on the throne, who liveth forever and ever.

REV. 7:12 Saying, Amen: Blessing, and glory, and wisdom, and thanksgiving, and honour, and power, and might, (be) unto our God forever and ever. Amen.

REV. 11:17 Saying, We give thee thanks, O Lord God Almighty, which art, and wast, and art to come; because thou hast taken to thee thy great power, and hast reigned.

REV. 12:12 Therefore rejoice, (ye) heavens, and ye that dwell in them. Woe to the inhabiters of the earth and of the seal for the devil is come down unto you, having great wrath, because he knoweth that he hath but a short time.

REV. 22:7 Behold, I come quickly: blessed (is) he that keepeth the sayings of the prophecy of this book.

AREA FIVE — CONSEQUENCES OF
NOT BEING THANKFUL

In the following two verses examine the consequences of not being thankful. It causes the loss of all things.

DEU 28:47 Because thou servedst not the Lord thy God with joyfulness, and with gladness of heart, for the abundance of all (things);
    48 Therefore shalt thou serve thine enemies which the Lord shall send against thee, in hunger, and in thirst, and in nakedness, and in want of all (things): and he shall put a yoke of iron upon thy neck, until he have destroyed thee.

AREA SIX — RESULTS OF
PRAISE AND THANKFULNESS

Notice how creative an attitude of thanks is. It precipitates the creative flow of God within our spirits. It brings forth the presence of God. It gives us strength. Yes, a negative mental attitude brings loss. A positive mental attitude brings gain.

2 CH 5:13 It came even to pass, as the trumpeters and singers (were) as one, to make one sound and be heard in praising and thanking the Lord; and when they lifted up (their) voice with the trumpets and cymbals and instruments of musick, and praised the Lord, (saying), For (he is) good; for his mercy (endureth) forever: that (then) the house was filled with a cloud, (even) the house of the Lord;

NEH 8:10 Then he said unto them, Go your way, eat the fat, and drink the sweet, and send portions unto them for whom nothing is prepared: for this day is holy unto our Lord: neither by ye sorry; for the joy of the Lord is your strength.

AREA SEVEN — JOY AND GLADNESS
ORIGINATE IN GOD

Examine the following verses to discover the source of our positive mental attitude. You will find it to be God. If I try to work up a positive mental attitude myself, rather than allowing it to be birthed in my spirit by Almighty God, then I have a dead work, which is sin, and needs to be repented of. However, we as Christians come to God as the source of all things and He births them within us. Therefore He is glorified.

1 CH 16:27 Glory and honour (are) in his presence; strength and gladness (are) in his place.

EZRA 6:22 And kept the feast of unleavened bread seven days with joy: for the Lord had made them joyful, and turned the heart of the king of Assyria unto them, to strengthen their hands in the work of the house of God, the God of Israel.

PSA 4:7 Thou hast put gladness in my heart, more than in the time (that) their corn and their wine increased.

PSA 16:11 Thou wilt shew me the path of life: in thy presence (is) fullness of joy; at thy right hand (there are) pleasures for evermore.

PSA 30:11 Thou hast turned for me my mourning into dancing: thou hast put off my sackcloth, and girded me with gladness;
        12 To the end that (my) glory may sing praise to thee, and not be silent. O Lord my God, I will give thanks unto thee forever.

PSA 48:2 Beautiful for situation, the joy of the whole earth, (is) mount Zion, (on) the sides of the north, the city of the great King.

PSA 51:12 Restore unto me the joy of thy salvation; and uphold me (with thy) free spirit.

PSA 90:14 O satisfy us early with thy mercy; that we may rejoice and be glad all of our days.

PSA 105:43 And he brought forth his people with joy, (and) his chosen with gladness:

PSA 107:1 O give thanks unto the Lord, for (he is) good: for his mercy (endureth) forever.

PSA 132:16 I will also clothe her priests with salvation: and her saints shall shout aloud for joy.

PSA 149:2 Let Israel rejoice in him that made him: let the children of Zion by joyful in their King.

PROV 10:22 The blessing of the Lord, it maketh rich, and he addeth no sorrow with it.

SOL 1:4 Draw me, we will run after thee: the king hath brought me into his chambers: we will be glad and rejoice in thee, we will remember thy love more than wine: the upright love thee.

ISA 51:11 Therefore the redeemed of the Lord shall return, and come with singing unto Zion; and everlasting joy (shall be) upon their head: they shall obtain gladness and joy; (and) sorrow and mourning shall flee away.

ISA 55:12 For ye shall go out with joy, and be led forth with peace: the mountains and the hills shall break forth before you into singing, and all the trees of the field shall clap (their) hands.

ISA 56:7 Even them will bring to my holy mountain, and make them joyful in my house of prayer: their burnt offerings and their sacrifices (shall be) accepted upon mine altar; for mine house shall be called an house of prayer for all people.

ISA 60:15 Whereas thou hast been forsaken and hated, so that no man went through (thee), I will make thee an eternal excellency, a joy of many generations.

ISA 61:3 To appoint unto them that mourn in Zion, to give unto them beauty for ashes, the oil of joy for mourning, the garment of praise for the spirit of heaviness; that they might be called trees of righteousness, the planting of the Lord, that he might be glorified.
   10 I will greatly rejoice in the Lord, my soul shall be joyful in my God; for he hath clothed me with the garments of salvation, he hath covered me with the robe of righteousness, as a bridegroom decketh (himself) with ornaments, and as a bride adorneth (herself) with her jewels.

ISA 65:18 But be ye glad and rejoice for ever (in that) which I create: for, behold, I create Jerusalem a rejoicing, and her people a joy.

JER 15:16 Thy words were found, and I did eat them; and thy word was unto me the joy and rejoicing of mine heart: for I am called by thy name, O Lord God of hosts.

JOEL 2:23 Be glad then, ye children of Zion, and rejoice in the Lord your God: for he hath given you the former rain moderately, and he will cause to come down for you the rain, the former rain, and the latter rain in the first (month).

ZECH 2:10 Sing and rejoice, O daughter of Zion: for, lo, I come, and I will dwell in the midst of thee, saith the Lord.

JOHN 16:24 Hitherto have ye asked nothing in my name: ask, and ye shall receive, that your joy may be full.

JOHN 17:13 And now come I to thee; and these things I speak in the world, that they might have my joy fulfilled in themselves.

ACTS 13:52 And the disciples were filled with joy, and with the Holy God, (even) thy God, hath anointed thee with the oil of gladness above

ACTS 14:17 Nevertheless he left not himself without witness, in that he did good, and gave us rain from heaven, and fruitful seasons, filling our hearts with food and gladness.

ROM 14:17 For the kingdom of God is not meat and drink; but righteousness, and peace, and joy in the Holy Ghost.

ROM 15:13 Now the God of hope fill you with all joy and peace in believing, that ye may abound in hope, through the power of the Holy Ghost.

GAL 5:22 But the fruit of the Spirit is love, joy, peace, long suffering, gentleness, goodness, faith,
    23 Meekness, temperance: against such there is no law.

1 TH 1:6 And ye became followers of us, and of the Lord, having received the word in much affliction, with joy of the Holy Ghost:

PHM 1:20 Yea, brother, let me have joy of thee in the Lord: refresh my bowels in the Lord.

HEB 1:9 Thou hast loved righteousness, and hated iniquity; therefore God, (even) thy God, hath anointed thee with the oil of gladness above thy fellows.

JUD 1:24 Now unto him that is able to keep you from falling, and to present (you) faultless before the presence of his glory with exceeding joy.

MY PERSONAL REFLECTIONS ON A POSITIVE MENTAL ATTITUDE

By Mark Virkler

God is the light; satan is the darkness. God is the edifier; satan is the accuser. God is the giver of good life; satan is the thief who comes to rob, kill and destroy. God is the One who frees us from condemnation, satan is the adversary, throwing challenging thoughts constantly into our minds.

When I understood these contrasting titles of God and satan, and that satan is the accuser and God the Comforter, I began in my mind to discern the origin of accusative thoughts and comforting thoughts. I found that approximately 80 percent of my thought processes were accusative, and only about 20 percent were based in comfort. Therefore I discovered that I was unwittingly giving over much of my thought processes to satan. As my prayer life was deepened through communion with God, so that I experienced two-way dialogue with God during my prayer times, I found that God was constantly telling me to come to peace, to believe, to hope, that He was working all things after the counsel of His will. I found Him to be encouraging, loving, edifying, lifegiving, positive, and optimistic. I found Him to be a much less judgmental God than I had theologically framed Him to be. Instead, He was just like the Jesus of Nazareth Whom I had come to love. The best way to describe Him was incomprehensible love.

As I have surveyed several hundred people who have also learned to experience God through two-way prayer, I have discovered that 100 percent of them have also found out that God is much more loving and less judgmental than they had previously thought Him to be when they had simply reasoned about Him theologically. It reminds me of what Jesus said: "You search the Scriptures because you think that in them you will have life but you are **unwilling to come to me,** that you might have life." Many Christians are so boxed in by the rationalism of our time that they no longer have direct Spirit-to-spirit encounter with Almighty God, as was recorded from Genesis to Revelation in the Holy Bible.

What I have found is that laws and theology often produce death, while direct Spirit encounter produces life. As I have communed with God I have discovered He has turned me (along with thousands of others) from a pessimist to an optimist, from a grumbler to a worshipper, from fearful to faithful, from a doubter to one who is full of hope.

My own experience and the experience of thousands of others has demonstrated that personal encounter with God changes negative mental attitudes to positive ones. It is clear from the several hundred verses that have preceded this statement, that God is committed to our **dwelling on** "whatever is true, whatever is honorable, whatever is right, whatever is pure, whatever is lovely, whatever is of good repute, if there is any excellence and if anything worthy of praise, let your mind dwell on these things (Phil. 4:8)."

WORLDVIEW — ADVANCING LIGHT OR ADVANCING DARKNESS?

By Mark Virkler

Finally we come to the worldview being expressed not only by Dave Hunt, but by much of fundamentalism at this time. It was the worldview I held for many years, but now have begun to discard. It is the view that things are destined to get worse and worse rather than better and better. It is a worldview that prophesies gloom and darkness, rather than glory and light. It has begun to strike me as strange that the living organism that is the light of the world, essentially prophesies darkness to the world.

However there is another worldview beginning to permeate the evangelical church. That is the belief that the light is going to conquer the darkness, rather than the darkness overcoming the light. It is the view that Christ is incarnate in His church, establishing the kingdom, bringing the kingdoms of this world under the dominion of the kingdom of God. It is the belief that Christ is working through the hands, feet, hearts, minds and mouths of the Church, establishing His kingdom on earth as it is in heaven.

If you have never searched through Scripture looking for the verses that delineate this worldview, asking God to give you a spirit of revelation (Eph. 1:18), I encourage you to do so now, using the following concordance study of the word **kingdom** as your base of study. As the Bereans, examine the scriptures eagerly to see if **these things BE SO.** Look for whatever truth you can find that would substantiate this other worldview.

It seems that as we review church history we see that God has constantly brought to the light new emphases and insights from the Holy Scriptures. Often rather than searching Scripture for the truth of this new insight, we have instead sought to **prove it wrong,** and gone on to stone the prophets. Let us not continue to make this same mistake which is recorded over and over for us in Scripture. Instead let us "pay attention to the prophetic word . . . as to a lamp shining in a dark place, until the day dawns and the morning star arises in our hearts." (II Pet. 1:19).

Following are some questions for which you may want to find answers.

1. We have included numerous verses that can be used to help define "kingdom" as used in Scripture. As you go through this concordance study you will find a number of verses therein which you will be able to use to gain a clear definition of the usage of this word kingdom. Also for your benefit we have included many verses describing God's power over all the kingdoms of this world. I urge you to consider the significance of this great truth.

a. Define the word "kingdom" used in Scripture.
b. Define the relationship of the kingdoms of this world to God
c. Define the relationship of the kingdoms of this world to the Kingdom of God.

2. Define the Kingdom of God.
   a. Its current location
   b. Its current goal and mission
   c. Its source of power
   d. Its ultimate revealing
   e. Its current relationship to the other kingdoms of this world.

3. After a careful study of the first verse of Revelation, how much of that book do you believe should be taken symbolically? How much should be taken literally?

4. You may want to examine the concept of **both** advancing light *and* advancing darkness, and discern how these concepts inter relate.

Index: **KINGDOM (250 References)**
Title: *The Two World Views*
Range: **GENESIS 1:1 to REVELATION 22:21**

To assist you in your study we have broken the following 250 verses on kingdom into six areas. They are:

1. Kingdom as defined and used in scripture.
2. The relationship of the kingdoms of this world to God.
3. Defining the Kingdom of God.
4. Entrance into and position in the Kingdom of God.
5. The current revealing and location of the Kingdom of God.
6. The ultimate revealing and the Kingdom of God.

AREA ONE — KINGDOM AS DEFINED AND USED IN SCRIPTURE

From the following verses define kingdom as you see it being used in Scripture. I would see it as essentially synonomous with nation. It is one's sphere of influence. Therefore I believe we may have a kingdom of drama, a kingdom of arts, a kingdom of economics, kingdoms in the field of education. A kingdom is a sphere of influence.

EXO 19:5 Now therefore, if ye will obey my voice indeed, and keep my covenant, then ye shall be a peculiar treasure unto me above all people: for all the earth (is) mine:

6 And ye shall be unto me a kingdom of priests, and an holy nation. These (are) the words which thou shalt speak unto the children of Israel.

DEU 17:18 And it shall be, when he sitteth upon the throne of his kingdom, that he shall write him a copy of this law in a book of (that which is) before the priests the Levites:

DEU 28:25 The Lord shall cause thee to be smitten before thine enemies: thou shalt go out one way against them, and flee seven ways before them: and shalt be removed into all the kingdoms of the earth.

2 SA 7:12 And when thy days be fulfilled, and thou shalt sleep with thy fathers, I will set up thy seed after thee, which shall proceed out of thy bowels, and I will establish his kingdom.

13 He shall build an house for my name, and I will stablish the throne of his kingdom forever.

1 KI 4:21 And Solomon reigned over all kingdoms from the river unto the land of the Philistines, and unto the border of Egypt: they brought presents, and served Solomon all the days of his life.

1 KI 9:5 Then I will establish the throne of thy kingdom upon Israel forever, as I promised to David thy father, saying, There shall not fail thee a man upon the throne of Israel.

1 KI 21:7 And Jezebel his wife said unto him, Dost thou now govern the kingdom of Israel? arise, (and) eat bread, and let thine heart be merry: I will give thee the vineyard of Naboth the Jezreelite.

2 KI 19:19 Now therefore, O Lord our God, I beseech thee, save thou us out of his hand, that all the kingdoms of the earth may know that thou (art) the Lord God, (even) thou only.

1 CH 14:2 And David perceived that the Lord had confirmed him king over Israel, for his kingdom was lifted up on high, because of his people Israel.

2 CH 17:10 And the fear of the Lord fell upon all the kingdoms of the lands that (were) round about Judah, so that they made no war against Jehoshaphat.

EST 5:3 Then said the king unto her, What wilt thou, queen Esther? and what (is) thy request? it shall be even given thee to the half of the kingdom.

ISA 19:2 And I will set the Egyptians against the Egyptians: and they shall fight every one against his brother, and every one against his neighbour; city against city, (and) kingdom against kingdom.

MAT 4:8 Again, the devil taketh him up into an exceeding high mountain, and sheweth him all the kingdoms of the world, and the glory of them;

LUK 4:5 And the devil, taking him up into an high mountain, shewed unto him all the kingdoms of the world in a moment of time.

AREA TWO — THE RELATIONSHIP OF THE KINGDOMS OF THIS WORLD TO GOD

In this section determine how effective and complete is God's rule amongst the kingdom of men. Did God wind up the universe and then let it go on its own, or is He ruling over the realm of mankind. Who establishes and pulls down kingdoms? Who gives kingdoms unto various men, and who removes them? I believe you will agree that it is the living God who rules in the realm of mankind, and giveth it to whomsoever he will.

1 KI 11:11 Wherefore the Lord said unto Solomon, Forasmuch as this is done of thee, and thou hast not kept my covenant and my statutes, which I have commanded thee, I will surely rend the kingdom from thee, and will give it to thy servant.
13 Howbeit I will not rend away all the kingdom; (but) will give one tribe to they son for David my servant's sake, and for Jerusalem's sake which I have chosen.
31 And he said to Jeroboam, Take thee ten pieces for thus saith the Lord, the God of Israel, Behold, I will rend the kingdom out of the hand of Solomon, and will give ten tribes to thee:
34 Howbeit I will not take the whole kingdom out of his hand: but I will make him prince all the days of his life for David my servant's sake, whom I chose, because he kept my commandments and my statutes:
35 But I will take the kingdom out of his son's hand, and will give it unto thee, (even) ten tribes.

1 CH 22:9 Behold, a son shall be born to thee, who shall be a man of rest; and I will give him rest from all his enemies round about; for his name shall be Solomon, and I will give peace and quietness unto Israel in his days.
10 He shall build an house for my name; and he shall be my son, and I (will be) his father; and I will establish the throne of his kingdom over Israel forever.

2 CH 1:1 And Solomon the son of David was strenghtened in his kingdom, and the Lord his God (was) with him, and magnified him exceedingly.

2 CH 17:5 Therefore the Lord stablished the kingdom in his hand; and all Judah brought to Jehoshaphat present; and he had riches and honour in abundance.

2 CH 20:6 And said, O Lord God of our fathers, (art) not thou God in heaven? and rulest (not) thou over all the kingdoms of the heathen? and in thine hand (is there not) power and might, so that none is able to withstand thee?

2 CH 20:29 And the fear of God was on all the kingdoms of (those) countries, when they had heard that the Lord fought against the enemies of Israel.

2 CH 36:22 Now in the first year of Cyrus king of Persia, that the word of the Lord (spoken) by the mouth of Jeremiah might be accomplished, the Lord stirred up the spirit of Cyrus king of Persia, that he made a proclamation throughout all his kingdom, and (put it) also in writing, saying,
     23 Thus saith Cyrus king of Persia, All the kingdoms of the earth hath the Lord God of heaven given me; and he hath charged me to build him an house in Jerusalem, which (is) in Judah. Who (is there) among you of all his people? The Lord his God (be) with him, and let him go up.

EZR 1:1 Now in the first year of Cyrus king of Persia, that the word of the Lord by the mouth of Jeremiah might be fulfilled, the Lord stirred up the spirit of Cyrus king of Persia, that he made a proclamation throughout all his kingdom, and (put it) also in writing, saying,
     2 Thus saith Cyrus king of Persia, The Lord God of heaven hath given me all the kingdoms of the earth; and he hath charged me to build him an house at Jerusalem, which (is) in Judah.

PSA 22:28 For the kingdom (is) the Lord's: and he (is) the governor among the nations.

PSA 45:6 Thy throne, O God, (is) forever and ever: the sceptre of thy kingdom (is) a right sceptre.

PSA 103:19 The Lord hath prepared his throne in the heavens; and his kingdom ruleth over all.

ISA 23:11 He stretched out his hand over the sea, he shook the kingdoms: the Lord hath given a commandment against the merchant (city), to destroy the strong holds thereof.

ISA 60:12 For the nation and kingdom that will not serve thee shall perish; yea, (those) nations shall be utterly wasted.

JER 1:10 See, I have this day set thee over the nations and over the kingdoms, to root out, and to pull down, and to destroy, and to throw down, to build, and to plant.

JER 18:7 At what instant I shall speak concerning a nation, and concerning a kingdom, to pluck up, and to pull down, and to destroy (it);

8 If that nation, against whom I have pronounced, turn from their evil, I will repent of the evil that I thought to do unto them.

9 And (at what) instant I shall speak concerning a nation, and concerning a kingdom, to build and to plant (it);

DAN 4:3 How great (are) his signs! and how mighty (are) his wonders! his kingdom (is) an everlasting kingdom, and his dominion (is) from generation to generation.

17 This matter (is) by the decree of the watchers, and the demand by the word of the holy ones: to the intent that the living may know that the most High ruleth in the kingdom of men, and giveth it to whomsoever he will, and setteth up over it the basest of men.

18 This dream I king Nebuchadnezzar have seen. Now thou, O Belteshazzar, declare the interpretation thereof, forasmuch as all the wise (men) of my kingdom are not able to make known unto me the interpretation: but thou (art) able; for the spirit of the holy gods (is) in thee.

25 That they shall drive thee from men, and thy dwelling shall be with the beasts of the field, and they shall make thee to eat grass as oxen, and they shall wet thee with the dew of heaven, and seven times shall pass over thee, till thou know that the most High ruleth in the kingdom of men, and giveth it to whomsoever he will.

29 At the end of twelve months he walked in the palace of the kingdom of Babylon.

30 The king spake, and said, Is not this great Babylon, that I have built for the house of the kingdom by the might of my power, and for the honour of my majesty?

31 While the word (was) in the king's mouth, there fell a voice from heaven, (saying), O king Nebuchadnezzar, to thee it is spoken; The kingis departed from thee.

32 And they shall drive thee from men, and thy dwelling (shall be) with the beasts of the field: they shall make thee to eat grass as oxen, and seven times shall pass over thee, until thou know that the most High ruleth in the kingdom of men, and giveth it to whomsoever he will.

34 And at the end of the days I Nebuchadnezzar lifted up mine eyes unto heaven, and mine understanding returned unto me, and I blessed the most High, and I praised and honoured him that liveth forever, whose dominion (is) an everlasting dominion, and his kingdom (is) from generation to generation:

36 At the time my reason returned unto me; and for the glory of my kingdom, mine honour and brightness returned unto me; and my counsellors and my lords sought unto me; and I was established in my kingdom, and excellent majesty was added unto me.

DAN 5:18 O thou king, the most high God gave Nebuchadnezzar thy father a kingdom, and majesty, and glory, and honour:
    21 And he was driven from the sons of men; and his heart was made like the beasts, and his dwelling (was) with the wild asses: they fed him with grass like oxen, and his body was wet with the dew of heaven; till he knew that the most high God ruled in the kingdom of men, and (that) he appointeth over it whomsoever he will.
    26 This (is) the interpretation of the thing: MENE, God hath numbered thy kingdom, and finished it.
    28 PERES; Thy kingdom is divided and given to the Medes and Persians.

DAN 6:26 I make a decree, that in every dominion of my kingdom men tremble and fear before the God of Daniel: for he (is) the living God, and stedfast forever, and his kingdom (that) which shall not be destroyed, and his dominion (shall be even) unto the end.

AREA THREE — DEFINING THE KINGDOM OF GOD

Define the kingdom of God in as much detail as possible from the following verses. You will find that it is everlasting, and that God's dominion continues throughout all generations. It is not of this world. It is inner and spiritual — righteousness, and peace and joy in the Holy Spirit. It is not words but a demonstration of Divine power. It is like a small seed that is planted and grows, until it finally becomes a full sized tree. It is growing now.

1 CH 28:10 Take heed now; for the Lord hath chosen thee to build an house for the sanctuary: be strong, and do (it).
    CH 29:11 Thine, O Lord (is) the greatness, and the power, and the glory, and the victory, and the majesty: for all (that is) in the heaven and in the earth (is thine); thine (is) the kingdom, O lord, and thou art exalted as head above all.

PSA 145:13 Thy kingdom (is) an everlasting kingdom, and thy dominion (endureth) throughout all generations.

ISA 9:6 For unto us a child is born, unto us a son is given: and the government shall be upon his shoulder: and his name shall be called Wonderful, Counselor, the mighty God, The everlasting Father, The Prince of Peace.
    7 Of the increase of (his) government and peace (there shall be)

no end, upon the throne of David, and upon his kingdom, to order it, and to establish it with judgment and with justice from henceforth even for ever. The zeal of the Lord of hosts will perform this.

MAT 6:13 And lead us not into temptation, but deliver us from evil: For thine is the kingdom, and the power, and the glory, forever. Amen.

MAT 13:11 He answered and said unto them, Because it is given unto you to know the mysteries of the kingdom of heaven, but to them it is not given.

MAT 13:19 When any one heareth the word of the kingdom, and understandeth (it) not, then cometh the wicked (one), and catcheth away that which was sown in his heart. This is he which received seed by the way side.

MAT 13:24 Another parable put he forth unto them, saying, The kingdom of heaven is likened unto a man which sowed good seed in his field.

MAT 13:31 Another parable put he forth unto them, saying, The kingdom of heaven is like to a grain of mustard seed.

MAT 13:32 Which indeed is the least of all seeds: but when it is grown, it is the greatest among herbs, and becometh a tree, so that the birds of the air come and lodge in the branches thereof.
    33 Another parable spake he unto them; The kingdom of heaven is like unto leaven, which a woman took, and hid in three measures of meal, till the whole was leavened.

MAT 13:38 The field is the world; the good seed are the children of the kingdom; but the tares are the children of the wicked (one);

MAT 13:41 The Son of man shall send forth his angels, and they shall gather out of his kingdom all things that offend, and them which do iniquity;
    42 And shall cast them into a furnace of fire: there shall be wailing and gnashing of teeth.
    43 Then shall the righteous shine forth as the sun in the kingdom of their Father. Who hath ears to hear, let him hear.
    44 Again, the kingdom of heaven is like unto treasure hid in a field; the which when a man hath found, he hideth, and for joy thereof goeth and selleth all that he hath, and buyeth that field.
    45 Again, the kingdom of heaven is like unto a merchant man,

seeking goodly pearls:

46 Who, when he had found one pearl of great price, went and sold all that he had, and bought it.

47 Again, the kingdom of heaven is like unto a net, that was cast into the sea, and gathered of every kind:

MAT 13:52 Then said he unto them, Therefore every scribe (which is) instructed unto the kingdom of heaven is like unto a man (that is) an householder, which bringeth forth out of his treasure (things) new and old.

MAT 18:23 Therefore is the kingdom of heaven likened unto a certain king, which would take account of his servants.

LUK 1:33 And he shall reign over the house of Jacob forever, and of his kingdom there shall be no end.

JOH 18:36 Jesus answered, My kingdom is not of this world: if my kingdom were of this world, then would my servants fight, that I should not be delivered to the Jews: but now is my kingdom not from hence.

ROM 14:17 For the kingdom of God is not meat and drink; but righteousness, and peace, and joy in the Holy Ghost.

1 CO 4:20 For the kingdom of God (is) not in word, but in power.

AREA FOUR — ENTRANCE INTO AND POSITION IN THE KINGDOM OF GOD

In these verses examine how one enters into the kingdom of God. How is one's position established in the kingdom? You will find that we must become as little children, simple, straightforward, honest. We must see our spiritual need. We must seek and cherish this inner experience of God. When we are rich financially, it is hard to see and desire this inner walk. It is a kingdom where servanthood brings leadership.

MAT 5:3 Blessed (are) the poor in spirit: for theirs is the kingdom of heaven.

MAT 5:10 Blessed (are) they which are persecuted for righteousness' sake: for theirs is the kingdom of heaven.

MAT 5:19 Whosoever therefore shall break one of these least commandments, and shall teach men so, he shall be called the least in the kingdom of heaven: but whosoever shall do and teach (them), the same shall be called great in the kingdom of heaven.

20 For I say unto you, That except your righteousness shall exceed (the righteousness) of the scribes and Pharisees, ye shall in no case enter into the kingdom of heaven.

MAT 6:33 But seek ye first the kingdom of God, and his righteousness; and all these things shall be added unto you.

MAT 7:21 Not every one that saith unto me, Lord, Lord, shall enter into the kingdom of heaven; but he that doeth the will of my Father which is in heaven.

MAT 11:11 Verily I say unto you, Among them that are born of woman there hath not risen a greater than John the Baptist: notwithstanding he that is least in the kingdom of heaven is greater than he.

12 And from the days of John the Baptist until now the kingdom of heaven suffereth violence, and the violent take it by force.

MAT 18:1 At the same time came the disciples unto Jesus, saying, Who is the greatest in the kingdom of heaven?

3 And said, Verily I say unto you, Except ye be converted, and become as little children, ye shall not enter into the kingdom of heaven.

4 Whosoever therefore shall humble himself as this little child, the same is greatest in the kingdom of heaven.

MAT 19:14 But Jesus said, Suffer little children, and forbid them not, to come unto me: for of such is the kingdom of heaven.

MAT 19:23 Then said Jesus unto his disciples, Verily I say unto you, That a rich man shall hardly enter into the kingdom of heaven.

24 And again I say unto you, It is easier for a camel to go through the eye of a needle, than for a rich man to enter into the kingdom of God.

MAT 20:1 For the kingdom of heaven is like unto a man (that is) an householder, which went out early in the morning to hire labourers into his vineyard.

MAT 20:21 And he said unto her, What wilt thou? She saith unto him, Grant that these my two sons may sit, the one on thy right hand, and the other on the left, in my kingdom.

MAT 21:31 Whether of them twain did the will of (his) father? They say unto him, The first. Jesus saith unto them, Verily I say unto you, That the publicans and the harlots go into the kingdom of God before you.

MAT 23:13 But woe unto you, scribes and Pharisees, hypocrites! for ye shut up the kingdom of heaven against men: for ye neither go in (yourselves), neither suffer ye them that are entering to go in.

MAR 9:47 And if thine eye offend thee, pluck it out: it is better for thee to enter into the kingdom of God with one eye, than having two eyes to be cast into hell fire:

MAR 10:14 But when Jesus saw (it), he was much displeased, and said unto them, Suffer the little children to come unto me, and forbid them not: for of such is the kingdom of God.
15 Verily I say unto you, Whosoever shall not receive the kingdom of God as a little child, he shall not enter therein.

MAR 10:23 And Jesus looked round about, and saith unto his disciples, How hardly shall they that have riches enter into the kingdom of God!
24 And the disciples were astonished at his words. But Jesus answereth again, and saith unto them, Children, how hard is it for them that trust in riches to enter into the kingdom of God!
25 It is easier for a camel to go through the eye of a needle, than for a rich man to enter into the kingdom of God.

LUK 9:62 And Jesus said unto him, No man, having put his hand to the plough, and looking back, is fit for the kingdom of God.

LUK 18:16 But Jesus called them (unto him), and said, Suffer little children to come unto me, and forbid them not: for of such is the kingdom of God.
17 Verily I say unto you, Whosoever shall not receive the kingdom of God as a little child shall in no wise enter therein.

LUK 18:24 And when Jesus saw that he was very sorrowful, he said, How hardly shall they that have riches enter into the kingdom of God!
25 For it is easier for a camel to go through a needle's eye, than for a rich man to enter into the kingdom of God.

2 PE 1:11 For so an entrance shall be ministered unto you abundantly into the everlasting kingdom of our Lord and Saviour Jesus Christ.

AREA FIVE — THE CURRENT REVEALING AND LOCATION OF THE KINGDOM OF GOD

How and where is the kingdom of God being manifested now? In heaven? On earth? Both? After the kingdom of iron (Dan. 2:41) God was going to set up a kingdom which will never be destroyed. I believe He did that by planting a seed in Jesus' death, which was then coupled with power in Acts 2, and now is growing into a mighty tree, ruling over the kingdoms of this world. Christ came preaching about his kingdom, saying it was at hand, and healing all manner of sickness and disease. He taught us to command it forth "Thy kingdom come, Thy will be done. . ." (imperatives in Greek). Jesus said that when He cast out devils by the Spirit of God, then the kingdom of God is come unto us. It is a kingdom that cometh not with observation, but it is God within you (Lk. 17:21). We have been translated from the power of darkness, into the kingdom of His dear Son (Col. 1:13). We **have received** a kingdom (Heb. 12:28). As the tree grows the kingdoms of this world are actually taken back under the domain of the Kingdom of God (Rev. 11:15).

DAN 2:37 Thou, O king, (art) a king of kings: for the God of heaven hath given thee a kingdom, power, and strength, and glory.

    39 And after thee shall arise another kingdom inferior to thee, and another third kingdom of brass, which shall bear rule over all the earth.

    40 And the fourth kingdom shall be strong as iron: forasmuch as iron breaketh in pieces and subdueth all (things): and as iron that breaketh all these, shall it break in pieces and bruise.

    41 And whereas thou sawest the feet and toes, part of potters' clay, and part of iron, the kingdom shall be divided; but there shall be in it of the strength of the iron, forasmuch as thou sawest the iron mixed with miry clay.

    42 And (as) the toes and feet (were) part of iron, and part of clay, (so) the kingdom shall be partly strong, and partly broken.

    44 And in the days of these kings shall the God of heaven set up a kingdom, which shall never be destroyed: and the kingdom shall not be left to other people, (but) it shall break in pieces and consume all these kingdoms, and it shall stand forever.

DAN 7:14 And there was given him dominion, and glory, and a kingdom, that all people, nations, and languages, should serve him: his dominion (is) an everlasting dominion, which shall not pass away, and his kingdom (that) which shall not be destroyed.

    16 I came near unto one of them that stood by, and asked him the truth of all this. So he told me, and made me know the interpreta - tion of the things.

18 But the saints of the most High shall take the kingdom, and possess the kingdom forever, even for ever and ever.

22 Until the Ancient of days came, and judgment was given to the saints of the most High; and the time came that the saints possessed the kingdom.

23 Thus he said, The fourth beast shall be the fourth kingdom upon earth, which shall be diverse from all kingdoms, and shall devour the whole earth, and shall tread it down, and break it in pieces.

24 And the ten horns out of this kingdom (are) then kings (that) shall arise: and another shall rise after them; and he shall be diverse from the first, and he shall subdue three kings.

25 And he shall speak (great) words against the most High, and shall wear out the saints of the most High, and think to change times and laws: and they shall be given into his hand until a time and times and the dividing of time.

26 But the judgment shall sit, and they shall take away his dominion, to consume and to destroy (it) unto the end.

27 And the kingdom and dominion, and the greatness of the kingdom under the whole heaven, shall be given to the people of the saints of the most High, whose kingdom (is) an everlasting kingdom, and all dominions shall serve and obey him.

MAT 3:2 And saying, Repent ye: for the kingdom of heaven is at hand.

MAT 4:17 From that time Jesus began to preach, and to say, Repent: for the kingdom of heaven is at hand.

MAT 4:23 And Jesus went about all Galilee, teaching in their synagogues, and preaching the gospel of the kingdom, and healing all manner of sickness and all manner of disease among the people.

MAT 6:10 Thy kingdom come. Thy will be done in earth, as (it is) in heaven.

MAT 9:35 And Jesus went about all the cities and villages, reaching in their synagogues, and preaching the gospel of the kingdom, and healing every sickness and every disease among the people.

MAT 10:7 And as ye go, preach, saying, The kingdom of heaven is at hand.

MAT 12:28 But if I cast out devils by the Spirit of God, then the kingdom of God is come unto you.

MAT 16:28 Verily I say unto you, There be some standing here, which shall not taste of death, till they see the Son of man coming in his kingdom.

MAR 1:14 Now after that John was put in prison, Jesus came into Galilee, preaching the gospel of the kingdom of God,

15 And saying, The time is fulfilled, and the kingdom of God is at hand: repent ye, and believe the gospel.

MAR 4:26 And he said, So is the kingdom of God, as if a man should cast seed into the ground;

MAR 4:30 And he said, Whereunto shall we liken the kingdom of God? or with what comparison shall we compare it?

MAR 9:1 And he said unto them, Verily I say unto you, That there be some of them that stand here, which shall not taste of death, till they have seen the kingdom of God come with power.

MAR 12:34 And when Jesus saw that he answered discreetly, he said unto him, Thou art not far from the kingdom of God. And no man after that durst ask him (any question).

LUK 4:43 And he said unto them, I must preach the kingdom of God to other cities also: for therefore am I sent.

LUK 8:1 And it came to pass afterward, that he went throughout every city and village, preaching and shewing the glad tidings of the kingdom of God: and the twelve (were) with him,

LUK 8:10 And he said, Unto you it is given to know the mysteries of the kingdom of God: but to others in parables; that seeing they might not see, and hearing they might not understand.

LUK 9:2 And he sent them to preach the kingdom of God, and to heal the sick.

LUK 9:11 And the people, when they knew (it), followed him: and he received them, and spake unto them of the kingdom of God, and healed them that had need of healing.

LUK 9:27 But I tell you of a truth, there be some standing here, which shall not taste of death, till they see the kingdom of God.

LUK 9:60 Jesus said unto him, Let the dead bury their dead: but go thou and preach the kingdom of God.

LUK 10:9 And heal the sick that are therein, and say unto them, The kingdom of God is come high unto you.
11 Even the very dust of your city, which cleaveth on us, we do wipe off against you: nothwithstanding be ye sure of this, that the kingdom of God is come nigh unto you.

LUK 11:2 And he said unto them, When ye pray, say, Our Father which art in heaven, Hallowed by thy name. Thy kingdom come. Thy will be done, as in heaven, so in earth.

LUK 11:20 But if I with the finger of God cast out devils, no doubt the kingdom of God is come upon you.

LUK 12:31 But rather seek ye the kingdom of God; and all these things shall be added unto you.
32 Fear not, little flock; for it is your Father's good pleasure to give you the kingdom.

LUK 13:18 Then said he, Unto what is the kingdom of God like? and whereunto shall I resemble it?
19 It is like a grain of mustard seed, which a man took, and cast into his garden; and it grew, and waxed a great tree; and the fowls of the air lodged in the branches of it.
20 And again he said, Whereunto shall I liken the kingdom of God?
21 It is like leaven, which a woman took and hid in three measures of meal, till the whole was leavened.

LUK 16:16 The law and the prophets (were) until John: since that time the kingdom of God is preached, and every man presseth into it.

LUK 17:20 And when he was demanded of the Pharisees, when the kingdom of God should come, he answered them and said, The kingdom of God cometh not with observation:
21 Neither shall they say, Lo here! or, lo there! for, behold, the kingdom of God is within you.

LUK 23:42 And he said unto Jesus, Lord, remember me when thou comest into thy kingdom.
43 And Jesus said unto him, Verily I say, unto thee, today shalt thou be with me in paradise.

ACT 1:3 To whom also he shewed himself alive after his passion by many infallible proofs, being seen of them forty days, and speaking of the things pertaining to the kingdom of God:

ACT 8:12 But when they believed Philip preaching the things concerning the kingdom of God, and the name of Jesus Christ, they were baptized, both men and women.

ACT 14:22 Confirming the souls of the disciples, (and) exhorting them to continue in the faith, and that we must through much tribulation enter into a kingdom of God.

ACT 19:8 And he went into the synagogue, and spake boldly for the space of three months, disputing and persuading the things concerning the kingdom of God.

ACT 20:25 And now, behold, I know that ye all, among whom I have gone preaching the kingdom of God, shall see my face no more.

ACT 28:23 And when they had appointed him a day, there came many to him into (his) lodging; to whom he expounded and testified the kingdom of God, persuading them concerning Jesus, both out of the law of Moses, and (out of) the prophets, from morning till evening.

ACT 28:31 Preaching the kingdom of God, and teaching those things which concern the Lord Jesus Christ, with all confidence, no man forbidding him.

JOH 3:3 Jesus answered and said unto him, Verily, verily, I say unto thee, Except a man be born again, he cannot see the kingdom of God.

JOH 3:5 Jesus answered, Verily, verily, I say unto thee, Except a man be born of water and (of) the Spirit, he cannot enter into the kingdom of God.

COL 1:13 Who hath delivered us from the power of darkness, and hath translated (us) into the kingdom of his dear Son:

HEB 12:28 Wherefore we receiving a kingdom which cannot be moved, let us have grace, whereby we may serve God acceptably with reverence and godly fear:

AREA SIX — THE ULTIMATE REVEALING
OF THE KINGDOM OF GOD

As you read these verses, you may want to look up some of the contextual verses surrounding them in scripture. Decide what you believe concerning the ultimate revealing of the kingdom of God. I believe that at the end of this age Christ will deliver up the kingdom to God the Father, having finally put down all rule and all authority and power (I Co. 15:24). He will do this through His body, the Church, and His Holy Spirit. The paradox of Christianity is what we are becoming what we are. We are the righteousness of Christ, yet we are working out our soul; salvation. God rules over all, yet Christ is busy through us, the Church putting down all evil power and authority. We are becoming what is. Probably this is a paradox that is impossible for us to completely understand.

MAT 25:1 Then shall the kingdom of heaven be likened unto ten virgins, which took their lamps, and went forth to meet the bridegroom.

MAT 25:34 Then shall the King say unto them on his right hand, Come, ye blessed of my Father, inherit the kingdom prepared for you from the foundation of the world:

MAT 26:29 But I say unto you, I will not drink henceforth of this fruit of the vine, until that day when I drink it new with you in my Father's kingdom.

MAR 14:25 Verily I say unto you, I will drink no more of the fruit of the vine, until that day that I drink it new in the kingdom of God.

LUK 22:16 For I say unto you, I will not any more eat thereof, until it be fulfilled in the kingdom of God.
    18 For I say unto you, I will not drink of the fruit of the vine, until the kingdom of God shall come.

1 CO 15:24 Then (cometh) the end, when he shall have delivered up the kingdom to God, even the Father; when he shall have put down all rule and all authority and power.

2 TI 4:1 I charge (thee) therefore before God, and the Lord Jesus Christ, who shall judge the quick and the dead at his appearing and his kingdom;

JAM 2:5 Hearken, my beloved brethren, Hath not God chosen the poor of this world rich in faith, and heirs of the kingdom which he hath promised to them that love him?

WORLDVIEW:
THE COMING REFORMATION

By Thomas Reid

Today a controversial issue confronts the evengelical community. It is called the "kingdom now" teaching. Its emphasis is to bring reformation to our sociological structure.

Pat Robertson stated in a recent interview in the **Buffalo News,** "The Church is moving from a millennial viewpoint to a kingdom-now philosophy." In his book, **The Secret Kingdom,** the dynamic head of the Christian Broadcasting Network challenges the Christians of America to develop a kingdom mentality that will create Christian servants. These servants will then bring productive change to our social structure.

The purpose of this article is to look at the teaching of contemporary evangelical leaders who claim a kingdom-now emphasis. We will also look at the questions they raise for serious-minded evangelicals who desire to establish a biblical worldview.

The problem is this: many evangelicals and Pentecostals have not developed an adequate worldview. Instead, they have reacted to the liberals within the established denominations who have attempted to bring reformation to society by purely political and humanistic means.

David Chilton in **Paradise Restored** notes that those who successfully colonized the New World "were expecting the New World would be Christianized. They were certain of victory. They knew that Christians are destined for dominion." Chilton goes on to state: "Examples could be multiplied in every field. The whole rise of Western Civilization — science and technology, medicine, the arts, constitutionalism, the jury system, free enterprise, literacy, increasing productivity, a rising standard of living, the high status of women — *is attributable to one major fact: the West has been transformed by Christianity.*"

No evangelical would deny this fact. In spite of that knowledge, though, evangelicals did not develop a theological position concerning the church's responsibility to society. However, something dramatic is happening to the theology and philosophical outlook of some evangelicals today.

Jeremy Rifkin states in his provocative book **The Emerging Order** that "at this very moment a spectacular change in Christian theology is taking place, virtually unnoticed. The change itself is simple, but basic. The ramifications are extraordinary. God's very first commandment to human-kind in the book of Genesis is being redefined. Its redefinition changes the entire relationship of human beings to both God and the temporal world."

Rifkin's "unnoticed" has become increasingly "noticed." We can hardly have a Moral Majority among us, without developing a theology of responsibility for social change. Perhaps the greatest single cultural force in American life today is the evangelical / neo-Pentecostal community.

So why no theology for social reformation? Perhaps a look at evangelicals' recent history would answer that question.

A fatalistic view of the world has been shaped by an emphasis on the escape of the church from earth's problems through a "rapture" — without a constant balancing of the responsibility of the church to sociological reformation.

Kingdom-now teachers maintain that the "rapture mentality" has philosophically paralyzed evangelicalism. Many evangelicals envision the world getting worse and worse, the church becoming weaker, until the redeemed are salvaged at the last minute by the rapture of the church out of the chaotic social and spiritual confusion of last-day apostasy.

Many kingdom-now teachers remain, as I do, premillennialists. They maintain a belief in a rapture, tribulation, Armageddon and millennial reign. However, their new emphasis is on the responsibility the church has today to both society and to the planet. Also they hold a viewpoint that the church will experience the greatest awakening in the history of Christianity and will arise both in proclamation as well as in demonstration by lifestyle as a witness of God's kingdom on planet earth.

Recent concepts have contributed to either a fatalistic or monastic attitude among other evangelicals, not the least of which is our modern emphasis on science. The rather recent discovery of the law of thermodynamics has shaped the philosophical view of the world held by some evangelicals. The second law of thermodynamics states that all matter and energy were created in this original state with an order and value to them. That ordered state is continually being eroded by an irreversible natural process. According to this law of entropy, all matter and energy are constantly and without exception moving from an ordered to a disordered state.

Many evangelicals have basically embraced this scientific view of matter and have applied it to society, with an attendant fatalism.

Most evangelicals grew up within the confines of small, anemic, minority churches that were largely impotent insofar as changing the world was concerned. Now evangelicals have awakened to a world in which they have power, prestige and ability to bring about sociological change.

Those who teach kingdom-now hold that evangelicals must develop a theology of sociological responsibility or we will again permit the liberals in Protestantism and the liberation theologians in Catholicism to shape our world — while we go merrily along awaiting the rapture. We need to remember how the church in Russia found itself "arguing about the color of the drapes in the cathedral" while the atheists were building a newly reformed society around them.

John Naisbitt in his best-seller **Megatrends** warns us concerning the major trend in our society of change from hierarchies to networking. Hierarchies (which include denominations) are largely controlled by a pyramid structure. Hierarchies have been praised and blamed, but never replaced. Naisbitt states, "Hierarchies remain; our belief in their efficiency does not."

There are three million people in the United States associated with Pentecostalism's largest denomination, the Church of God in Christ. The Assemblies of God is second with fewer than two million. However, Gallup tells us there are more than 15 million in unaligned charismatic churches. Now those independents are beginning to network.

Under the direction of Charles Green of New Orleans, the Network of Christian Ministries was organized with men such as Kenneth Copeland and John Gimenez on the executive board. Their mission is to bring the millions of charismatics together in a networking relationship.

Oral Roberts has formed another networking group called Charismatic Bible Ministries. Copeland and Gimenez are on that board also along with 25 other leaders with 50 more being added as trustees.

This places the institutional hierarchy in Pentecostalism on the defensive. Within networking there is room for a variety of theological and philosophical opinions. In the hierarchy, that scope is considerably limited.

Naisbitt predicts that the response of the hierarchy is to make the pyramid even stronger. In the terms of denominationalism, it is predictable that Pentecostal denominations will utilize such doctrinal issues as eschatology and its attendant worldview to create a more impregnable structure. The inevitable reaction will be, as it has been in the past, a major shift in both ministries, churches and individuals from the hierarchy to the network.

Can the thinking of denominations be reshaped to embrace the huge reformation that is about to take place? If not, my fear is that Pentecostal denominations will be seriously affected in the move toward networking now taking place.

How could evangelicals and Pentecostals, who had always held to a monastic and fatalistic view of the world, be involved in both reformation of society and social action?

Evangelicals can point to Jerry Falwell who formed the Moral Majority. Pentecostals can point to David Wilkerson who began Teen Challenge, a rehabilitation project for drug addicts.

THEOLOGY OF THE EARTH
What is the meaning of the Garden of Eden? Why did God say not only to "tend the garden" but also to "subdue the earth?" Was it not possible that the beginning of the recreation process only pinpointed the geographical location of the garden, and God's commission and purpose

for the human race was to extend the "kingdom" or the "reign of God" to all the earth?

If this is true, it presupposes that the Bible is the handbook for man's dominion over the earth. A systematic theology of dominion over the earth would then result from a study of the total context of Scripture.

Upon that premise we begin to form a "theology of the earth.'

Why did Jesus say the meek shall inherit the earth? Why does the book of Romans say, "God promised Abraham and his descendants that the world would belong to him" (Rom. 4:13,TEV)? Why did Jesus constantly emphasize, "Thy kingdom come on earth"? And why did the psalmist say, "The earth is the Lord's and the fullness thereof; the world, and they that dwell therein" (Ps. 24:1)?

Is there not contained in Scripture a theology of the earth that mandates a biblical view of ecology, economy, government, arts and society in general?

Is then God's mandate to Adam applicable to the church today?

The covenant that God made with Abraham had to do with the earth and is indicative of the covenant that Abraham's seed, the church, has with the earth. If this is true, then it is important for the church to bring about a reformation in the sociological structure as well as to recognize a biblical ecological mandate.

If we do not respond, we will leave that mandate for the humanists and the liberals.

KINGDOM THEOLOGY

Genesis and Colossians form a theological framework for a theology of dominion and a biblical basis for Christian responsibility.

The first truth in Colossians 1 is that all the "visible" or "material" universe over which God "reigns" is the kingdom of God. That "visible" includes every planet, star, constellation, or, as the writer states, "things in earth, and things in heaven."

Paul describes the kingdom of God as being "invisible." The invisible is defined as a governmental system of thrones, dominions, principalities and powers, which rule over the visible universe.

Into this governmental system came a rebellion. Lucifer led one third of the angels (the ruling delegated authorities of God), and perhaps also one third of the stars (visible material heavenly bodies) into the rebellion. He set up the capital city of this new kingdom of darkness on planet earth, which the Bible identifies as the "gates of hell."

Paul then speaks of the "reconciliation of things in heaven and things in earth," and notes they are redeemed through the blood of the cross. The purpose of this redemptive process seems to be to bring the entire material universe again under the total reign of God.

How is this to transpire? Paul links that victory not to Christ's future coming, but to His past victory on the cross. He is seen as the kinsman redeemer purchasing back the earth and the rebel material universe with His own blood. However the victory is not yet complete.

It seems reasonable that when the capital city (earth) falls to King Jesus, the rest of the visible kingdom (things in heaven) will also be reconciled. That is kingdom theology in a nutshell.

How will this be accomplished? Will the physical return of Christ be the only major focal point of this reconciliation, or does the church play a major role in the "occupying" process of the capital city of darkness.

Adam's purpose was to recapture for the King the rebellious capital city (planet earth) by subduing it. He failed, falling instead into the rebel camp. The second Adam (Christ) was born into the planet, and His very announcement was that the kingdom of God or the reign of God was here. And He gave His disciples all power (or delegated authority).

To illustrate: we, the church, are like the military forces (delegated authority) the queen of England sent to the Falkland Islands to regain lost territory. We are the king's delegated authority to reclaim the planet for our king.

If this is true then one of the great purposes of the church is to infiltrate the fabric of our society and bring a witness of Christ's kingdom to the kingdoms of this world. This is what Jesus meant by "occupy (for take territory) till I come."

KINGDOM LIFESTYLE

What did Jesus mean when He announced, "The kingdom of God is at hand" (Mark 1:15)? Is the lifestyle of kingdom law as outlined by Christ reserved only for a millennial reign, or can we live as overcomers in a kingdom lifestyle now?

I submit that kingdom lifestyle is available for God's people today. It involves the following:

First, *a throne,* Jesus our king indicated that the one who serves is the one who rules. The throne of His kingdom is therefore a servant's throne. Those who could be kings in His kingdom must learn to be servants. Any truly successful businessman knows that only by serving customer, supplier and employee can you truly succeed.

Second, kingdom lifestyle includes a *cross.* When Jesus said to take up our cross and follow Him, He was not referring to Calvary but rather to purpose in life. For Him the cross was His purpose. Therefore, our cross in His kingdom is the purpose for wihch we were born.

Third, if we rule from a throne of servanthood, and we have a purpose in life, we will be *productive.*

A productive society is a kingdom society.

Fourth, a kingdom lifestyle involves *creativity.* A person who relies on the power of the Holy Spirit will have creative ideas as did Daniel when God gave him the power to solve difficult problems.

Finally, if a person is a servant, has a purpose and is productive and creative, he will *prosper.*

These five ingredients of a kingdom lifestyle will not only affect our lives but will enable us to be a creative force of change in our society.

Jesus, when confronted with the question of the "when" of the kingdom, noted that the emphasis was to be only on the indwelling of the Spirit.

If the kingdom of God is within us, then the purpose of that creative power within is not only to win souls or get us to heaven, or take us up in the rapture, but to play a Daniel role in our society. We are to stand beside the kingdoms of this world and bring productive change to our society, through our demonstration of kingdom lifestyle.

THEOLOGY OF THE CHURCH

Kingdom-now proponents call us to examine the church as being the body of Christ programmed for victory and not defeat.

Jesus said, "Ye are the salt of the earth...the light of the world...a city set on a hill." He said, "Let you light so shine before men, that they may see your good works, and glorify your Father which is in heaven" (Matt. 5;13-16).

This is no less than a mandate for the social transformation of the world. What Jesus condemns is ineffectiveness, or the failing of Christians to change the society around us.

This theology of dominion does not destroy any particular eschatological position. One can believe in pre-tribulation rapture and the premillennial return of Christ and still hold to an eschatology of dominion.

But let us not lose sight of the purpose of the church to advance and take territory from satan and make ready for the rapture of the church, and the final return of the king and His church to set up the kingdom fully.

The church is programmed for success. We will affect the world to such an extent that the greatest revival in the history of the world will take place in the very last days. The final conflict will not be the result of an anemic church being rescued at the very end, but rather the conflict created by the power of a church in the midst of revival influencing all the world.

We *must* make ready the world for Christ's coming.

The ayatollah could not return to Iran until his followers had sufficiently prepared the nation for his return.

In a profoundly deeper way, the church must prepare the earth for the return of Jesus Christ. So the church must be called to repentance, maturity and a spirituality that will influence the world, bring the proclamation and demonstration of the kingdom to all nations — and then shall the end come.

The bride must mature so that the Bridegroom will come back to a mature bride who has both proclaimed and demonstrated the kingdom of God to the earth as a witness.

The church has a divine, biblical mandate to bring sociological reformation. To do this, the church must not only feel a social responsibility and develop a social consciousness but must develop this as a theological foundation upon which ministry is built.

This requires the leadership of godly people in every area of society.

God calls attention to lack of such leadership in Ezekiel 22. Here God looks for a man who would make up a wall, on behalf of the land. When He finds no man, He is forced to send destruction.

The gap is caused by ungodly priests, ungodly prophets, ungodly political leaders and ungodly business people. Notice, the decaying sociological structure which would be judged by God was created by spiritual people not being present in the secular leadership of society.

Today's problems are the same. But kingdom-now teaches the godly followers of Jesus can enter society and solve the problems.

APPLYING THESE TRUTHS TO YOUR LIFE

By Mark Virkler

This manual has been largely theological, in that we have been seeking to offer a biblical response to certain issues raised in a fundamentalist rationalistic culture. However, the core of Christianity is not theology. It is a Person, a Being of agape love, a love that is incomprehensible to the finite mind. Therefore, I do not want to leave this study on a simply theological note.

It took me years to work my way through the mazes of conflicting evangelical theologies, and find the person of Christ at the center of it all. Finally I found **Him**. I experienced Him in direct, ongoing, inner encounter. I experienced His love, I saw His vision. I heard His voice speaking regularly within my heart. I felt His emotions being fused to mine. I found myself transcending myself, as I began to become all that He is within me. I became wiser than my wisdom. I became stronger than my strength. I became more righteous than my righteousness. I became more loving than my own capacity to love. I found that God had fused Himself to me and that I was becoming all that He is, as I lived out of the divine initiative that flowed within.

I had healed the problem that Jesus had spoken of (Jn. 5:39, 40). I had allowed the theology of the book (Bible) to set the parameters through which I might personally encounter the Living God in an ongoing way. I had broken free from my marriage to rationalism and analytical thought, and had begun to experience direct inner encounter through the Holy Spirit. I had broken free from the bondage of my culture, and returned to the balance of Jesus of Nazareth, my Lord and Savior, Who lived constantly out of the flow of God's vision, voice and power within Him (Jn. 5:19, 20, 30; 8:26,28,38). Not that Jesus threw away His mind in favor of direct spiritual encounter. He **used His heart and mind BOTH to their fullest capacity,** and that is what **we do, also.**

It is hard for the one who is married to his mind to respect and honor the one who has discovered Spirit impressions. It is so hard for the one who has learned to walk in the Spirit, to honor the one who lives in analytical thought. God gave us both our hearts and our minds so that we could live **comfortably in both.** That is where I seek to live (as this and all my other study manuals should demonstrate).

Life is much different now. Christianity is much different now. I live out of the flow of God within, rather than out of the limitations of my mind. I have found a **Person** amongst all the theology, Jesus my Lord and Savior.

MAY EACH ONE FIND HIM!

Communion with God

BY REV. MARK VIRKLER

An Alternative To **THE SEDUCTION OF CHRISTIANITY**

This 170 page study manual contains a thoroughly practical study on discerning God's Voice. It is designed to bring people into dialogue with Almighty God. Rather than close the door to direct Spirit-to-spirit encounter with God, this book teaches Christians how to effectively converse with Him. A survey of a recent group finishing this course revealed that 99% of the class had broken through into two-way communication with God in their prayer lives.

DR. RICHARD WATSON - Oral Roberts University

"COMMUNION WITH GOD" by Mark and Patti Virkler has dramatically changed my prayer life. I have found I can will to dialogue with Christ on a daily basis, and I do. I believe this inspired approach to be absolutely essential to the growth of every serious Christian. I further believe COMMUNION WITH GOD is an excellent example of the uniquely powerful way God is reaching out to His people today."

DR. PAUL YONGGI CHO

"Your thesis about logos and rhema is a masterpiece! Every minister in the world should read that from Dan to Beersheba." (This thesis by Dr. Fount Shults is bound together with the *COMMUNION WITH GOD* manual).

REV. THOMAS REID

"The course COMMUNION WITH GOD is going to change the nation by building a new generation of people that hear God's voice and dream God's dreams."

REV. MARK VIRKLER

"My heart burns with the vision of seeing the church transformed by bringing Christians into two-way communication with God in their prayer lives."

by
Tommy Reid
with
Doug Brendel

This is the story of one church and one preacher. But the principles it presents are universal.

You will identify with the frustrations and struggles of the successful minister, Tommy Reid, who felt unfulfilled in spite of his achievements.

THE EXPLODING CHURCH promises to unleash a powerful dynamic within you. You will discover from reading this book God's infallible formula for church growth and personal renewal.

- -

PLEASE RUSH TO ME:

____ Copies, at a $3.50 donation, of THE EXPLODING CHURCH.

Make checks payable to:
Full Gospel Tabernacle Books
3210 Southwestern Blvd.
Orchard Park, NY 14127

Name _____

Address _____

City, State, Zip _____

Change Your Life Through Spiritual Insight From....

- Dr. Paul Yonggi Cho
- Dr. Robert Schuller
- Dr. Tommy Reid

Plus 5 Other Christian Leaders!

$4.97 EXPAND YOUR HORIZON

Want to put your whole self in tip-top mental, physical and spiritual condition?

Ann Watt Wiechmann is tops in advice and know-how. She shares how to get in shape through the rotation diet. Blood pressures have fallen, arthritics have vastly improved under her guidance.

The choice is yours....

$3.97 GROW OR DIE

CONTACT US FOR INFORMATION ON BOOKING
A BIBLICAL RESPONSE SEMINAR IN YOUR AREA

In 6 Days

by C.H. McGowen, M.D.

A book that has served to explain
the active creation to over 50,000 readers.

FROM SON-RISE

$3.95

For a complete listing of our seminars, books and tapes, contact:

James W. Biros • Florence Biros

412-946-8334

SON-RISE
Publications & Distribution Co.

Rte. 3, P.O. Box 202
New Wilmington, PA 16142

"We aim to have HIS SON-rise in every heart."
